Explorations
with *TesselMania!*

Activities for Math and Art Classrooms

Jill Britton

Dale Seymour Publications®

Dedicated to Merle Silverman and Kevin Lee

Artwork on the Explore disk in the directories < reverse > and < tessart > was contributed by Brigette and Len Church, as well as by student artists Kristina Andrew, Andrew Bateman, Walter Britton, Kimberly Cawsey, Charlind Dary, Steve Dawson, Henry Furmonowicz, Jill Greenwood, Abby-Gail Hyldig, Lyda Kobylansky, Tanya McLain, Tara Reburn, Sharon Thomas, and Jared Watters.

The *TesselMania!*®-generated graphics in this publication were captured from the Windows® version of the software. Minor differences exist between the Macintosh® and Windows® screens. In the Macintosh® screen, the menu bar has no **Help** command, **Tessellation Magic** uses a black rather than a white background, the double-white and double-black colors are on opposite ends of the color palette, and so forth. This publication points out the differences only when actual procedures differ between the two versions.

Project Editor: Joan Gideon

Production Coordinator: Shannon Miller

Art: Jill Britton

Text and cover design: Lisa Klein, Pisa Design

Published by Dale Seymour Publications®, an imprint of Addison-Wesley Longman, Inc.

Order Number DS21808

ISBN 1-57232-270-5

1 2 3 4 5 6 7 8 9 10-ML-00 99 98 97 96

Contents

Contents

Disk Contents

Directory	Files to Accompany
polygons	Chapter 1
pixels	Chapter 2
tessart	Chapter 3
reverse	Chapter 4
sqgrids	Chapter 5
quilts#	Chapter 5
quilts	Chapter 5
islam#	Chapter 6
islam	Chapter 6

Introducing Tessellations with *TesselMania!*®

The *TesselMania!*® program was not designed to teach tessellations or transformational geometry. However, as you and your students complete these activities and access the files on the Explore disk, you will discover and use geometric transformations.

As you work through the activities and explore *TesselMania!*, you will be guided by graphics captured from the Windows version of the software. Minor differences exist between the Macintosh and Windows screens. On the Macintosh screen, you will see the menu bar has no **Help** command, **Tessellation Magic** uses a black rather than a white background, the double-white and double-black colors are on opposite ends of the color palette, and other small differences. This book points out differences only when actual procedures differ between the two versions.

The activities are presented in sequence. Skills learned and, in some cases, figures created in one activity are used in the next. You will need at least one computer, the *TesselMania!* software, a printed copy of each activity, and the Explore files (on disk or hard drive). You do not need prior experience with tessellations or electronic paint programs. You do need to be familiar enough with computers to run *TesselMania!*, to use a mouse, to use pull-down menus, and to access files. (Specific instructions for accessing files are not provided since these vary with the computer setup.)

Students may work through the activities independently or in pairs. The amount of guidance you need to provide will vary with the age, experience, and ability of your class. You may also lead the activities. A computer lab with a demonstration system consisting of a large color monitor or color LCD and a computer for every pair of students is an ideal setup. Several students per machine is workable. You can get by with just one computer and a demonstration system, as long as each student eventually gets the opportunity to access the software.

In this chapter, students learn to use the tools that modify the outline of a tile. Students do not use the *TesselMania!* paint tools yet, so they may focus on the tile outline, its geometric characteristics, and why it tessellates the plane. Once students find the paint tools, creating art becomes their objective—despite your good intentions to explore the geometry.

Before using *TesselMania!*, you may informally discuss tessellations. Ask your students where they have seen tilings. Use visual examples like floor tiles, quilts, or polygonal crackers—particularly varieties that include squares, rectangles, triangles, hexagons, and diamonds. On an overhead projector, compare a configuration of contiguous circles to a tessellation of squares. Point out the gaps between the circles. Comment on the absence of gaps in a tessellation, pointing out that the squares meet side to side and corner to corner.

Activity 1 · Introducing *TesselMania!*

As you explore the *TesselMania!* program, you will discover many interesting tessellations you can create. Start the program by double-clicking on its icon. You will see the logo screens and then the title screen. Three start-up options appear on the title screen. You may also easily get to these options from the menu bar.

For an introduction to tessellations, select **Instructions.** This option is also in the **Help** menu for Windows and in the **Options** menu for Macintosh. This book uses the form **(Menu): (Command)** to tell you which command to select in which menu (for example, **Options: Instructions**).

Read the first three pages of screen instructions, selecting **Next** to see the next screen. After the third page, select **Done.** (The information on the remaining eight pages will be presented in these activities.)

You can use the next option on the title screen, **Open** (also available from **File: Open**), to retrieve saved *TesselMania!* files such as the files on the Explore disk.

To begin a new tessellation, select the third option, **New,** or select **File: New.** The program asks you to choose the transformation or transformations *TesselMania!* will use to modify your tile. You may choose a single transformation—translation (slide), rotation (turn), or glide reflection (slide and flip)—by selecting one of the three choices in the top row. The choices in the bottom row give you the option to use a pair of transformations.

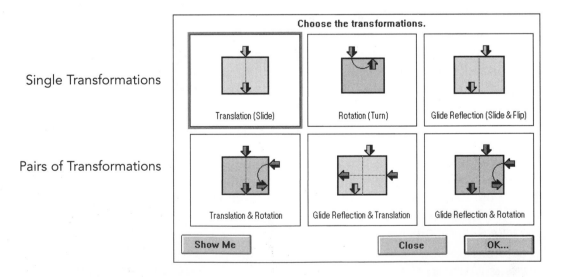

Double-click on **Translation.** (Since this option is framed, it has been selected by default. Selecting **OK** will also launch it.) You could have selected a different transformation or pair of transformations by clicking on it. Double-clicking both selects and launches a transformation type.

Once you have selected a transformation type, you must pick the type of tile to which *TesselMania!* will apply the transformation or transformations. The available choices depend upon the transformation type.

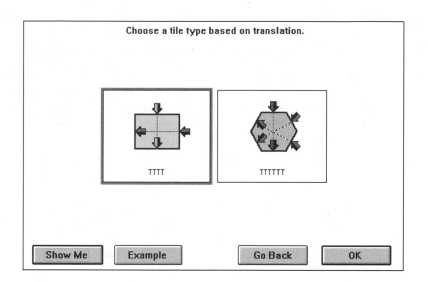

Double-click on the quadrilateral—or select **OK.** You are ready to begin creating a tessellation. A square tile is displayed in the window. As you complete the next 12 activities, you will change the outlines of tiles using just a few of the tools, function buttons, and commands in *TesselMania!*'s toolbox, command bar, and menu bar.

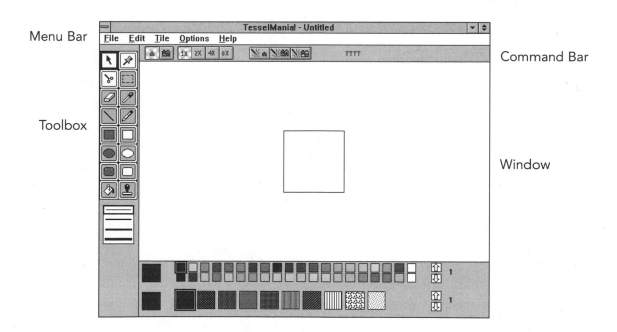

Show What You Have Learned

List the transformations (single transformations or pairs of transformations) that *TesselMania!* offers as choices. If you choose **Translation,** what are the choices you have for a tile type?

Activity 2 • Quadrilaterals and Translation

You are now ready to begin exploring tessellating shapes. Select **File: New.**
Double-click on **Translation** and then on the quadrilateral. Click on the
Tessellate button on the command bar. A tessellation of the square tile will fill
the window automatically. Like all tiles in a *TesselMania!*-generated tessellation,
the squares meet side to side and corner to corner.

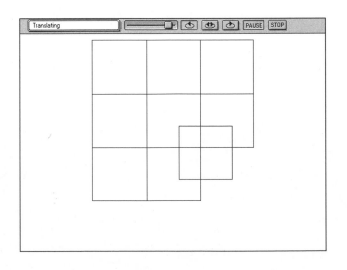

Click on the **Tessellation Magic** button on the command bar to watch
TesselMania! generate the tessellation. Since you selected translation as the
transformation type, the original tile slides to create the tessellation.

The command bar is now a control panel, which you can use to control
the speed and direction in any of *TesselMania!*'s magic or animation options.

The description on the left tells you what is happening in the animation—for example, "Translating." Change the animation speed by moving the slider bar. Click on the direction buttons to change the direction of the animation, and click on the **Pause** button to pause or renew the animation.

Slider Bar   Direction Buttons

Experiment with the slider bar, the direction buttons, and the **Pause** button. When you are done, click on the **Stop** button to stop the animation.

Now click on the **Edit Tile** button on the command bar (at the extreme left, next to the **Tessellate** button) to return to a single tile. Or use **Tile: Edit Tile.** (The same menu choice will read **Tessellate** when you are in single-tile mode.)

 Select **Edit Tile** any time you want to view or work with a single tile. In single-tile mode you get access to all of the tools in *TesselMania!*'s toolbox.

 Select **Tessellate** to see the window tessellated with a tile automatically. In tessellation mode, you can only use those tools that are used to change the outline of a tile (the **Arrow, Tack,** and **Scissors**).

Arrow   Tack   Scissors

 Return to single-tile mode. The **Arrow** tool is already selected for you. Click on the border of the tile with the point of the arrow. The handles that appear are what you will use to drag or stretch the tile.

Position the point of the arrow on a side of the tile; then drag the arrow (while holding the mouse button down) to drag the tile. You may move a tile at any time—but only in single-tile mode.

 Position the point of the arrow on a corner handle ▪, then drag the cursor (while holding the mouse button down, as usual) to s-t-r-e-t-c-h the square—horizontally or vertically—into an arbitrary rectangle.

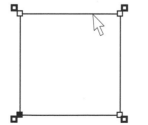

Select **Tessellate** to see a tessellation of the rectangle fill the window. Animate the tessellating process with the **Tessellation Magic** button. (**Tessellation Magic** can also be used in single-tile mode, but part of the tessellation will be covered by the palettes at the bottom of the screen.) Since the opposite sides of a rectangle are parallel and equal, any rectangle will tessellate by translation (sliding the tiles). When you are finished using a magic button, remember to stop the animation.

You deactivated the handles on the original tile when you selected **Tessellate.** This also happens if you click anywhere in the window except on the tile's border, in single-tile or tessellation mode.

If you remember the location of the original tile, click on its border with the arrow to reactivate its handles. Or click on the **Tack;** then select the **Arrow** (and click on the tile border for Macintosh) for the same effect.

Using a corner handle ◼, deform the original rectangle as before. What happens to the other rectangles? Put the point of the arrow on a vertex handle ◻; then drag the cursor diagonally. The rectangles will change into identical parallelograms.

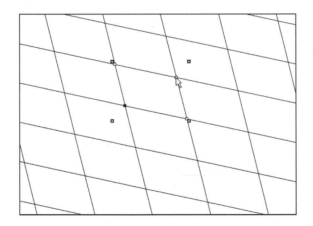

Animate the tessellating process with the **Tessellation Magic** button. Since the opposite sides of a parallelogram are parallel and equal, any parallelogram will tessellate by translation. Try changing the parallelogram more. The sides of the quadrilateral will remain parallel and equal. Otherwise, *TesselMania!* could not use translation to generate the tessellation.

Show What You Have Learned

Describe the different ways to activate the handles of a tile. How are the functions of the corner handles ◼ different from those of the vertex handles ◻? What kinds of quadrilaterals will tessellate by translation?

Activity 3 • Modifying a Tile Outline

In this activity, you will learn how to deform a tessellating polygonal tile by changing the contour of its sides. But first, you will learn to use other commands in the pull-down menus. If a command is available, it appears in bold type. Commands in dimmed type cannot be chosen. Commands are available when they are useful to what you are doing at a particular moment.

File   Edit   Tile   Options   Help

Select **File: New;** double-click on **Translation** and then on the quadrilateral. Activate the corners of the original square, and use them to change it into a parallelogram.

Select **Edit: Erase All** (**Erase All** in the **Edit** menu). What happens to the parallelogram? This command restores a tile outline to its original state so you can start over again.

Edit	
Undo	Ctrl+Z
Cut	Ctrl+X
Copy	Ctrl+C
Paste	Ctrl+V
Erase Painting	Ctrl+D
Erase All	

Select **Edit: Undo** and watch the effect on the tile. This command undoes your most recent action on a tile. If you want to undo an action, use **Undo** before you make any other changes. Select **Redo**—to undo your undo—or select **Erase All** again.

Deform the square into the parallelogram shown below by dragging its corner handles ■ and vertex handles □; then move the tile to the center of the window. (You may also move a tile using any corner marked with a ■.)

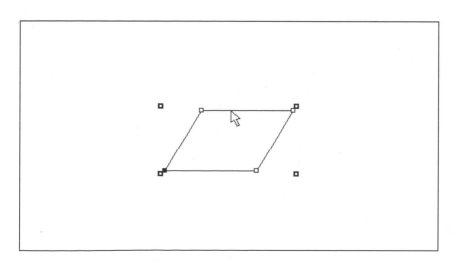

Select the **Tack** from the toolbox. When you reenter the window, your cursor will look like a tack. Position the point of the tack on an unmarked location on the upper edge of the parallelogram; then drag the tack. As you change one side, the opposite side will change as well. You determined which side would follow your changes (the related side) when you selected the transformation type. For translation, the related side is the parallel and equal opposite side.

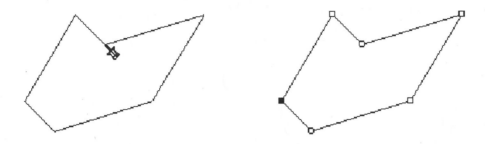

When you release the mouse button, two hollow circles appear on the tile—one where you clicked with the tack and the other in a corresponding position on the opposite side. For each point added, *TesselMania!* adds the corresponding second point.

Add some more points to change your tile again. You may make changes to any side. You can create curves by adding several points to a side.

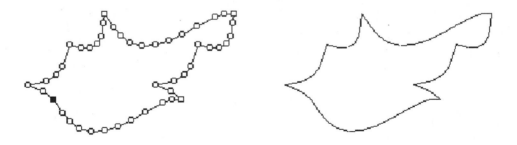

You can drag the new points using either the **Arrow** or **Tack.** *TesselMania!* will reject actions that won't work, such as dragging a point across the tile border. To delete a point you have added, use the **Scissors.** You won't be able to delete corners of the original polygon indicated by a □ or a ■. When you remove a point, *TesselMania!* removes the corresponding second point. To hide the points, select the **Arrow;** then click on any location not on the tile border.

Select **Tessellate;** then explore the three magic options on the command bar. As with **Tessellation Magic,** each can be used in either single-tile or tessellation mode. As before, control the animation with the slider bar, direction buttons, and **Pause** button. Click on **Stop** to stop the animation. (You may wish to explore the effect when **Options: Show Grid** is activated before you push a magic button. Turn off **Show Grid** when you are done.)

Select **Tile Magic** to watch *TesselMania!* construct your modified tile from its parent polygonal tile.

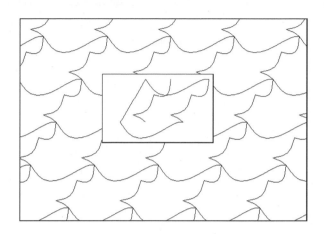

   Select **Tessellation Magic** to watch *TesselMania!* move your tile to generate the tessellation.

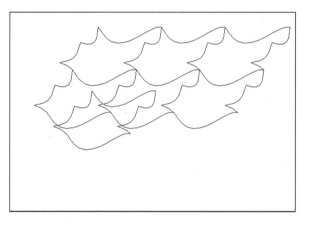

Select **Metamorphic Magic** to watch the evolution of your modified tile or tessellation into its parent tile or grid and then back again.

Show What You Have Learned

Explain how you can use the **Arrow, Tack,** and **Scissors.** Describe the effect of each of the magic options.

Activity 4 • Hexagons and Translation

In this activity, you will explore another tile that will tessellate by translation. Select **File: New,** double-click on **Translation,** then double-click on the hexagon.

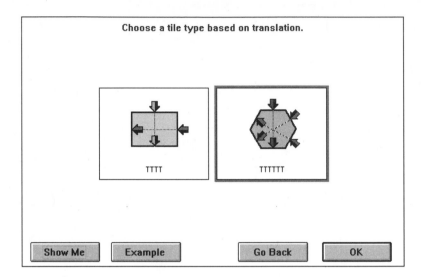

This tile is a regular hexagon. Select **Tessellate,** and watch the honeycomb tessellation fill the window. The hexagon tessellates because its sides are equal and each angle measures 120°. There are three angles at each corner. Three times 120° is 360°—the angles at each corner make a full circle with no gaps.

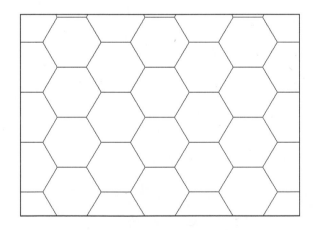

Animate the tessellating process with **Tessellation Magic**. *TesselMania!* generates the tessellation by sliding the initial tile until it is completely surrounded. The new tiles (which are all regular hexagons) slide into place like puzzle pieces because their opposite sides are parallel and equal.

Activate the handles of the original hexagon. Use them to deform this hexagon in all conceivable ways. *TesselMania!* automatically transmits your changes to all other hexagons in the tessellation. The opposite sides remain parallel and equal, otherwise translation could not be used.

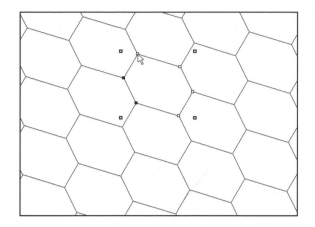

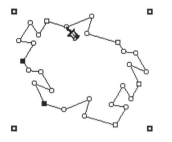

Return to single-tile mode. Add tack points to the sides of the hexagon with the **Tack**, and drag them to create interesting shapes. When you change a side, *TesselMania!* makes the corresponding change to the parallel and equal opposite side. Use **Tile Magic** to animate the construction of your modified tile from its parent hexagonal tile.

Select **Tessellate** and then the **Tack.** Drag the tack points in tessellation mode. As you make changes, the corresponding parallel and equal opposite side will also change—so will all other tiles in the tessellation. Experiment adding, dragging, and deleting tack points to see what happens.

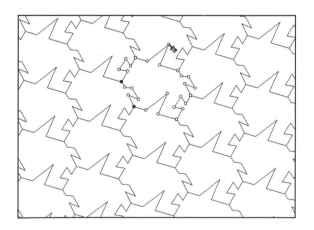

Show What You Have Learned

Look at the ways you can change the hexagon without changing the contour of the edge, and describe the characteristics of a hexagon that will tessellate by translation.

Activity 5 • Triangles and Midpoint Rotation

For some polygons, you can use rotation (turning about a point) to create tessellations.

In midpoint rotation, the shape turns about a point at the middle of one of its sides. In vertex rotation, the shape rotates about a corner (or vertex) into its place in the tessellation.

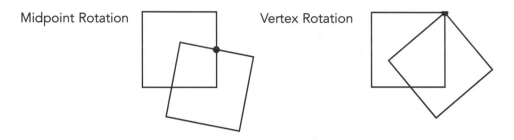

Midpoint Rotation   Vertex Rotation

In midpoint rotation, if you make a change to one half of a side, the change rotates 180° to the other half of the side. In vertex rotation, if you make a change to one side, the change rotates to an equal adjacent side.

In this activity, you will explore triangles and midpoint rotation. Select **File: New.** Begin by double-clicking on **Rotation;** then double-click on the triangle.

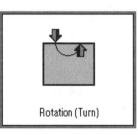

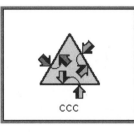

This tile is an equilateral triangle. Select **Tessellate,** and watch the tessellation fill the window. The triangle tessellates because its sides are equal and each angle measures 60°. Six 60° angles make a complete circle of 360°.

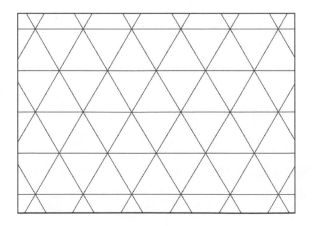

Activate the handles of the original triangle. The solid circles on the sides of the triangle are the midpoints of the sides. Deform this triangle in as many ways as you can. You can deform the tile into any triangle you wish—the tile still tessellates. This is because the sum of the measures of the three angles of the triangle does not change as it is deformed. You will discover that the sum is always 180° as it is in an equilateral triangle.

Now look at the window as a whole. Do you see three distinct sets of parallel lines crossing the screen? No matter how deformed your triangle is, these lines still appear parallel. In this activity, you will find out if they actually are parallel.

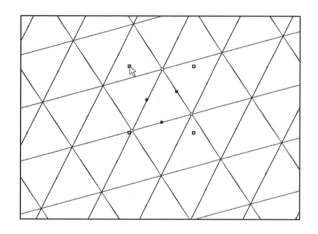

Select **File: Open,** then open the file < triang01 > in the < polygons > directory of the Explore disk.

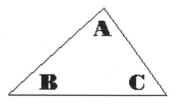

This is a scalene-triangle tile. Its angles have been labeled with the first three letters of the alphabet. These letters represent the measures of the angles as well.

Select **Tessellation Magic,** and watch the initial triangle rotate 180° about the midpoint of the side between angles *A* and *C*. Once the second triangle is in place, immediately click on **Pause.** Study the location of the six angles.

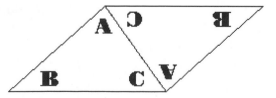

Because alternate angles (labeled either *A* or *C*) are equal, it follows from geometry that the quadrilateral made up of the two triangles is a parallelogram.

Click on **Stop;** then select **Tessellate.** Study the location of the various angles in the tessellation. Any two angles in alternate locations are the same size. All quadrilaterals consisting of two joined triangles are parallelograms. Therefore, this grid actually does consist of three distinct sets of parallel lines.

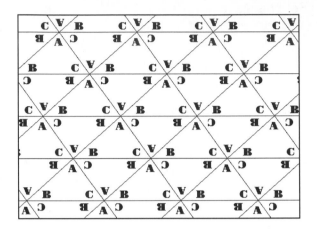

Notice that there are two of each angle, *A, B,* and *C,* surrounding every vertex. If the measures of two sets of the triangles' angles total 360°, then the measures of one set must total 180°. As a rule, *the sum of the angles in a triangle is always 180°.*

To the Teacher

Do not let students use **Tessellation Magic** beyond two tiles without an intervening hands-on activity. Regrettably, *TesselMania!* does not use midpoint rotation to generate the rest of the tessellation. The remaining tiles are positioned via equivalent transformations. Thus, since two successive 180° midpoint rotations result in an upright polygon, *TesselMania!* translates, rather than rotates, the initial triangle to position the third triangle. Since three successive 180° midpoint rotations result in an inverted polygon, the fourth triangle is positioned by rotating the initial triangle 180° about a vertex, and so on.

You may want to print the tessellation of labeled triangles by selecting **File: Print.** Give a copy to each student along with a pencil and tracing paper or a labeled cardboard polygon. Challenge students to come up with single transformations (midpoint rotation, vertex rotation, or translation) that will move the initial triangle to each of the 12 locations surrounding it. Use **Tessellation Magic** to confirm their choices. If a specific choice does not match the one actually used, then is it equivalent to it?

Select **Edit Tile** to return to single-tile mode; then select **Edit: Erase Painting.** This command erases anything you put inside the tile. If you had chosen **Erase All,** you would have erased all details and restored the tile outline to its original shape. Use this command in place of **File: New** to start over again using the same transformation and tile type.

Add tack points to half-sides of the triangle, and drag them in any appropriate direction. Your changes will be matched on the other half of the side you change. Use **Tile Magic** to watch *TesselMania!* construct your modified tile from its parent triangular tile. The modification to each half-side rotates 180° about the midpoint of the side to the related half-side.

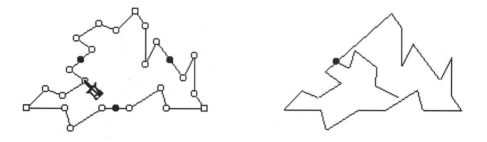

If you want to see the parent triangle while you work, select **Options: Show Grid** before selecting **Tile Magic.** Turn off **Show Grid** when you are done.

Select **Tessellate** and then the **Tack.** Drag the tack points in tessellation mode. Try adding, moving, and deleting tack points, but do not use **Tessellation Magic** until your teacher tells you to.

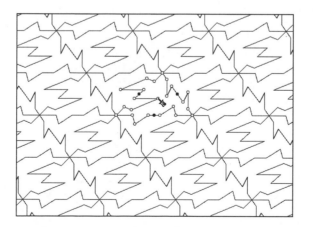

Show What You Have Learned

What property of triangles allows any triangle to tessellate by rotation about the midpoint of each of its sides? How does the tessellation show this property?

Activity 6 • Quadrilaterals and Midpoint Rotation

You may have noticed in Activity 5 that parallelograms, and thus rectangles and squares as well, will tessellate by midpoint rotation. Does this mean all quadrilaterals can tessellate by midpoint rotation? You'll find out in this activity.

Select **File: New.** Double-click on **Rotation;** then on the quadrilateral in the center of the first row of tiles.

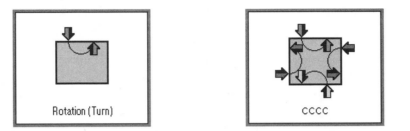

Select **Tessellation Magic,** and watch the initial square rotate 180° about the midpoint of one of its sides. Once the second square is in place, click on **Pause.** The third square could be positioned by rotating the second square 180° about the midpoint of another of its sides. This would turn the second square right-side up again. So, instead of using rotation, *TesselMania!* positions the third square by sliding the initial one. It positions the fourth by rotating the initial square 180° about the midpoint of another of its sides, and so on. Click on **Pause** and watch the counterclockwise progression of translations and midpoint rotations until the initial square is completely surrounded. Click on **Stop**.

Select **File: Open;** then open the file < quad01 > in the < polygons > directory on the Explore disk. Select **Tessellation Magic** again. Watch the four labeled angles of the square surround each vertex of the initial tile; then stop the animation. Select **Tessellate,** and study the tessellation. All vertices will be surrounded by the four angles of the square.

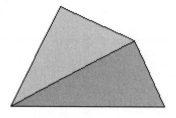

Open the file < quad02 > in the same directory. If you add a diagonal to a quadrilateral, you can subdivide its angles into the angles of two triangles. Since the angles of a triangle always total 180°, *the sum of the angles in a quadrilateral is always 360°.*

Open the file < quad03 >, then select **Tessellation Magic.** As you did with the square, watch the four labeled angles of the quadrilateral surround each corner of the initial tile; then stop the animation.

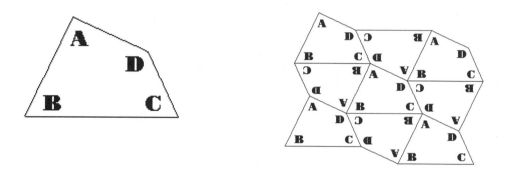

Now look at the tiles in tessellation mode. Look at each vertex: each one is surrounded by the four angles of the quadrilateral. Since the sum of the four angles in a quadrilateral is always 360°, the angles surrounding each vertex also total 360°—a complete circle. There are no gaps between tiles, so this is a true tessellation. You can conclude that any quadrilateral will tessellate by midpoint rotation.

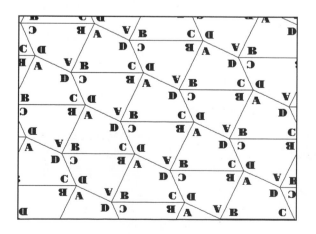

Select **Edit Tile** and then **Edit: Erase All.** Activate the square's handles, and explore with them. You will find you can deform the tile into any conceivable quadrilateral.

Select **Tessellate,** reactivate the handles of your quadrilateral, and deform it even more to see how the tessellation changes.

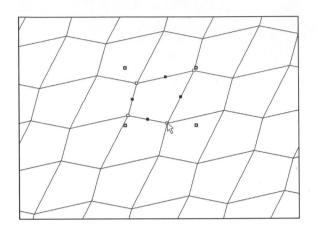

Back in single-tile mode, use the tack to change the tile's outline. Watch how the related half-sides match each other's modifications. Use **Tile Magic** to animate the construction of your modified tile from its parent tile.

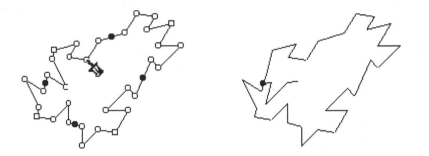

When you use the **Tack** in tessellation mode, you will be able to see how all the tiles' half-sides change as you drag tack points. Midpoint rotation can create wonderful tessellations!

Show What You Have Learned

What property of quadrilaterals allows any quadrilateral to tessellate by rotation about the midpoint of each of its sides? How does the tessellation show this property?

Activity 7 • Quadrilaterals and Vertex Rotation

A tessellating polygon may rotate about the midpoint of a side, as you saw in Activity 6. It can also rotate about one of its vertices (corners). Unfortunately, the current version of *TesselMania!* applies vertex rotation only to quadrilaterals and hexagons. (*TesselMania! Deluxe,* available only on CD-ROM, applies the transformation to equilateral triangles and isosceles triangles with apex angles of 90° or 120°.)

Open a new file and launch **Rotation;** then double-click on the quadrilateral at the far right of the first row of tiles.

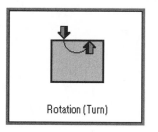

Rotation (Turn)

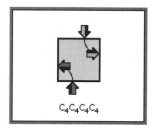

$C_4C_4C_4C_4$

Select **Tessellation Magic,** and watch the initial square rotate clockwise or counterclockwise about an appropriate vertex through angles of 90° or 180° (two 90° angles) until it is completely surrounded; then stop the animation.

Open the file < quad04 > in the < polygons > directory on the Explore disk. Select **Tessellate,** and then **Tessellation Magic** to watch four angles labeled either *B* or *D* surround two opposite vertices of the initial tile. Pause if you need to. (**Tessellation Magic** also works in single-tile mode, but the color and pattern palettes will cover the bottom of the screen.)

Four 90° angles make a complete circle of 360°. The vertices surrounded by these angles are said to be centers of four-fold rotational symmetry. After selecting **Stop,** study the tessellation. All corners involving angle *B* (or angle *D*) will be surrounded by exactly four of angle *B* (or angle *D*).

Return to single-tile mode; then use the **Tack** to modify the tile's outline. (Use distinct bumps or holes that do not disturb the angle labels.) A change to one side of the tile will be accompanied by a corresponding change to one of the equal adjacent sides (the related side). Use **Tessellation Magic** (in tessellation mode) to watch your changes to one arm of angle *B* or *D* rotate 90° about the vertex of the angle to its other arm.

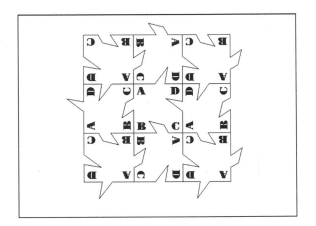

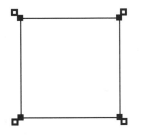

Use **Edit: Erase All** to return the tile to its original state. Activate the handles, and try to deform the quadrilateral. No matter what you do, it will remain a square—it has to so *TesselMania!* can use four rotations of 90° (fourfold rotation).

Select **Erase All** again; then select **Tessellate.** Use the **Tack** to explore how changes to the sides of the original square affect other tiles in the tessellation. Use **Tile Magic** if you wish to animate the construction of the modified tile from its parent square.

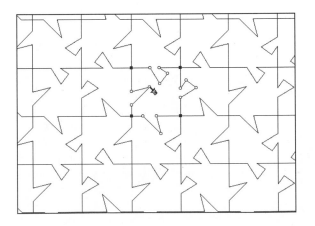

Clearly, if the angle of rotation is 90°, the quadrilateral must be a square. However, other angles of rotation are possible. Open a new file. Double-click on **Rotation;** then double-click on the quadrilateral at the far left of the second row of tiles.

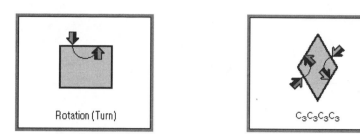

Select **Tessellate,** and study the configuration of tiles. The quadrilateral certainly appears to tessellate. Open the file < quad05 >. Select **Tessellation Magic** (in tessellation mode) to watch three angles labeled either *B* or *D* surround two opposite vertices of the initial tile. Pause when the initial tile is completely surrounded.

Both angle *B* and angle *D* must measure 360° ÷ 3 or 120°. The corresponding vertices are centers of three-fold rotational symmetry. In order for the quadrilateral to tessellate by vertex rotation, the arms of angle *B* or angle *D* must be equal. It follows that angles *A* and *C* are equal. Since the sum of the angles in a quadrilateral is always 360°, *A* and *C* must measure 60°. Since six 60° angles surround each of the other vertices of the quadrilateral, there are no gaps and the quadrilateral tessellates.

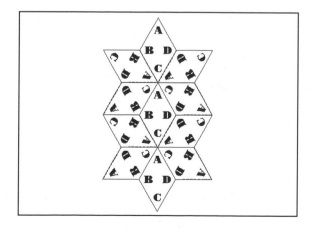

Click on **Stop,** return to single-tile mode, and select **Edit: Erase All.** If you activate the handles, you can alter the size of the quadrilateral but not its shape. Modify the sides of the tile with the **Tack**. Any change will be matched by a change to the related side. Explore the effect in tessellation mode if you wish.

Now try something different. Open a new file, and launch **Rotation** as before. This time, double-click on the quadrilateral in the center of the second row of tiles.

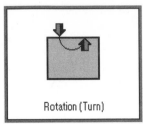

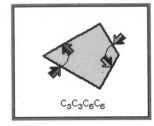

Look at the tiles in tessellation mode. Do they really tessellate? Open the file < quad06 >. Select **Tessellation Magic** (in tessellation mode) to watch three angles labeled *D* surround one vertex of the initial tile and six angles labeled *B* surround the opposite vertex. Pause when the initial tile is surrounded.

Angle *D* must measure $360° \div 3$ or $120°$. Angle *B* must measure $360° \div 6$ or $60°$. The corresponding vertices are centers of three-fold and six-fold rotational symmetry, respectively. Since the arms of angle *B* or angle *D* must be equal to allow vertex rotation, it follows that angles *A* and *C* are equal. Since the sum of the angles in a quadrilateral is always $360°$, *A* and *C* must measure $90°$. Since four $90°$ angles surround each of the other vertices of the quadrilateral, there are no gaps and the quadrilateral tessellates.

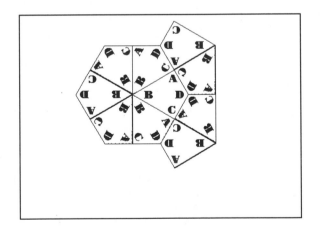

Click on **Stop**, return to single-tile mode, and select **Edit: Erase All.** Again, you may use the handles to alter the quadrilateral's size, but not its shape. Modify the tile outline with the **Tack** to see how related adjacent sides change. You can also modify the original tile in tessellation mode to explore the effect on the tessellation.

Show What You Have Learned.

Three kinds of quadrilaterals will tessellate by rotation about two opposite vertices. What characteristics of their angles or sides allow them to tessellate?

Activity 8 • Hexagons and Vertex Rotation

You have learned how quadrilaterals tessellate by rotating about a vertex. Triangles and hexagons with specific geometric properties will also tessellate this way. The current version of *TesselMania!* allows you to explore hexagons and vertex rotation—but not triangles.

Select **File: New,** double-click on **Rotation,** and then on the hexagon.

Rotation (Turn) $C_3C_3C_3C_3C_3C_3$

Select **Tessellation Magic,** and watch the initial regular hexagon rotate clockwise or counterclockwise about three of its vertices through an angle of 120° until it is completely surrounded. Stop the animation.

Select **Tessellate,** and watch the honeycomb tessellation fill the window. Activate the handles so you can deform the original hexagon. Be ruthless with your deformations! It may appear at first that you can deform the hexagon at will—but no matter what you do, you will not be able to change the magnitude of three of the polygon's angles.

Also, no matter how long or short you make the arms of these three angles, they will appear to remain equal. Clearly, there are geometric restrictions as to how you can deform the original hexagon.

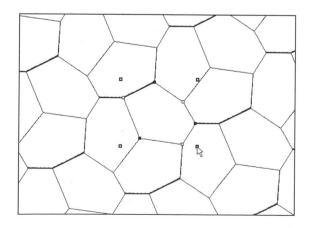

Open the file < hexag01 > in the < polygons > directory on the Explore disk. Select **Tessellate** and then **Tessellation Magic** to watch three of angle *B, D,* or *F* surround three vertices of the initial hexagon. Stop the animation.

Every corner involving an angle *B*, *D*, or *F* is surrounded by exactly three of the angle in question. Each of these angles must be 360° ÷ 3 or 120°. The corresponding vertices are centers of three-fold rotational symmetry.

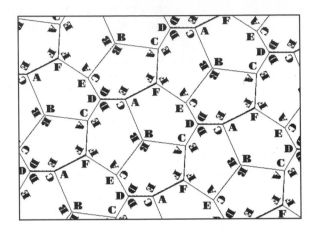

Use the **Tack** to modify the sides of the original hexagon while you observe the effect on the other tiles in the tessellation. With **Tessellation Magic,** you can watch your changes to one arm of angle *B*, *D*, or *F* rotate 120° about the vertex of that angle to its other arm. Clearly, the arms must be the same length. Otherwise vertex rotation would not work.

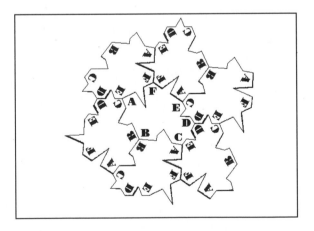

Stop the animation, and use **Tile Magic** to watch *TesselMania!* construct a single tile. The program rotates changes you made to one side of the hexagon through an angle of 120° to an equal adjacent side. The rotations are about alternate vertices of the hexagon.

Show What You Have Learned

Describe the characteristics of the angles and sides of a hexagon that will tessellate by rotation about three of its vertices.

Activity 9 • Quadrilaterals and Glide Reflection

In this activity, you will explore glide reflection—the last of *TesselMania!*'s single transformation types.

Open a new file. Click once on **Show Me** to see an animation of the current selection, **Translation.**

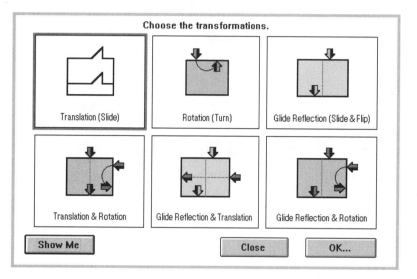

Now select **Glide Reflection,** and click on **Show Me.** You will see a change to one side of the polygon flip about or reflect in a dotted line and then slide to the opposite side. The direction of the slide will be parallel to the reflection line.

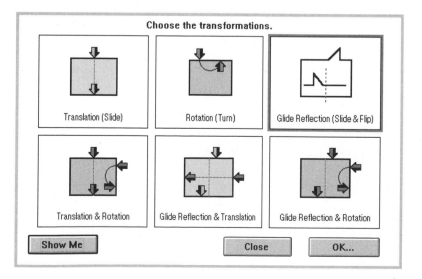

Launch **Glide Reflection.** You have two tile options—both quadrilaterals. If you select the quadrilateral on the left and then click on **Show Me,** *TesselMania!* will modify each of two adjacent sides of the polygon and move the change to the opposite side. If you select the quadrilateral on the right and click on **Show Me,** the program will modify each of two opposite sides and move the change to an adjacent side. The motion or transformation in both animations will be glide reflection. Launch the quadrilateral on the left.

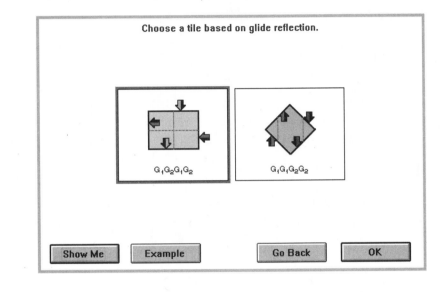

Choose a tile based on glide reflection.

$G_1G_2G_1G_2$ $G_1G_1G_2G_2$

Show Me   Example   Go Back   OK

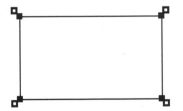
Activate the handles, and try to deform the quadrilateral. It will remain a rectangle. As you saw in earlier activities, the transformation type you choose puts geometrical restrictions on the polygon.

Open the file < quad07 > in the < polygons > directory on the Explore disk. Make changes to two adjacent sides of the tile with the **Tack.** Try to work around the angle labels. In this tile type, any change you make is also made to the equal and opposite side. Use **Tile Magic** to watch the modified tile form.

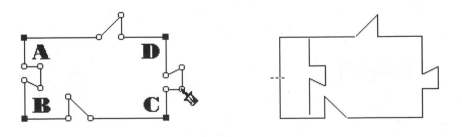

Now watch **Tessellation Magic** (in tessellation mode) until the initial tile is completely surrounded. You will see a dotted line, called a *perpendicular bisector,* cross the middle of the quadrilateral. *TesselMania!* positions the second tile by glide-reflecting the initial tile in the perpendicular bisector of the side between angles C and D. It positions every second tile thereafter by glide-reflecting the initial tile in the perpendicular bisector of one of its sides.

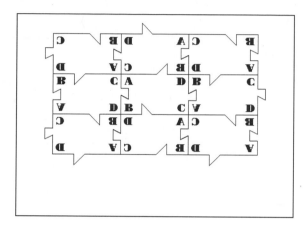

TesselMania! positions the remaining tiles by rotating the initial tile through an angle of 180° about a vertex. The effect is the same as two glide reflections, one right after the other. Rather than going around the block twice to get next door, the program takes a shorter route to do the same thing.

To make sure this rotation does indeed do the same thing as glide reflection, click on **Pause** as soon as the third tile is in place. Lay a sheet of acetate or tracing paper on top of the second tile—the one to the right of the initial tile— and trace the tile outline as well as the reversed letters. Flip the tile over from left to right—that is, reflect it in the perpendicular bisector of the side between angles B and C. Then slide it vertically upward until it coincides with the third tile. The angle labels will coincide as well. Click on **Stop.**

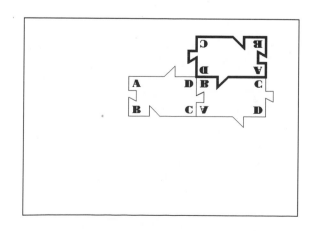

Open a new file and double-click on **Glide Reflection,** but this time launch the quadrilateral on the right.

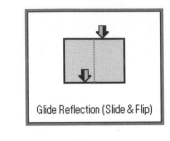

Glide Reflection (Slide & Flip)

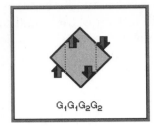

$G_1G_1G_2G_2$

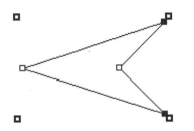

Activate the handles, and try to deform the quadrilateral. It will stay kite-shaped—either outward-bending (convex) or inward-bending (concave)—or it will collapse into a triangle.

Open the file < quad08 >. Modify two opposite sides of the tile. Any change you make is also made to the equal adjacent side. Use **Tile Magic** to see how each change is reflected in the line that passes through the midpoints of the two related sides.

Use **Tessellation Magic** (in tessellation mode) to watch the initial tile move until it is completely surrounded. Each of its vertices is surrounded by four angles—the four angles of the quadrilateral, which total 360°. *TesselMania!* positions every second tile by glide reflection. It positions the remaining tiles by translating the initial tile (equivalent to two glide reflections).

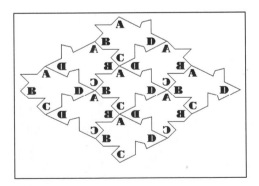

Show What You Have Learned

Describe the properties of the angles or sides of a quadrilateral that will tessellate by glide reflection.

Activity 10 • Translation and Midpoint Rotation

TesselMania! also offers transformations in pairs—translation and midpoint rotation, glide reflection and translation, and glide reflection and midpoint rotation.

Open a new file and launch **Translation & Rotation.** You have only one option. Use **Show Me** to see *TesselMania!* modify one side of the quadrilateral and translate it to the opposite side. Then changes to each of two half-sides rotate 180° about the midpoint of the side to the related half-side. Launch the quadrilateral.

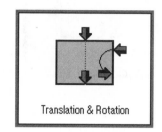

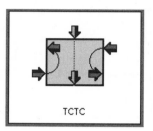

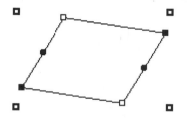

Activate the square's handles. No matter how you try to deform it, the quadrilateral will remain a parallelogram. For translation to work as a transformation, a polygon must have a pair of parallel and equal opposite sides.

Add tack points to sides and half-sides of the original parallelogram in tessellation mode. Experiment with *TesselMania!*'s magic options.

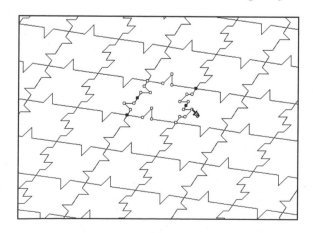

Show What You Have Learned

What kind of quadrilateral will tessellate by a combination of translation and midpoint rotation?

With *TesselMania!,* you can also combine translation with glide reflection.

Activity 11 • Glide Reflection and Translation

Open a new file, and launch **Glide Reflection & Translation.** Select **Show Me** to see *TesselMania!* modify one side of the quadrilateral, flip the change about a reflection line, and then slide it to the opposite side. Then a change to one of the remaining sides slides to the side opposite it. Launch the quadrilateral.

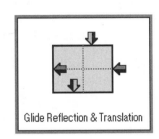

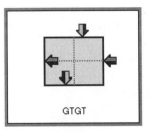

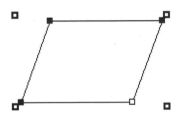

Activate the handles, and deform the quadrilateral. It will remain a parallelogram—as it did when you paired translation and midpoint rotation in Activity 10.

Using the tack, modify the sides of the original parallelogram in tessellation mode and watch the effect on all related sides. If you select **Tile Magic,** you will see the reflection line is perpendicular to the sides being transformed and passes through the center of the parallelogram.

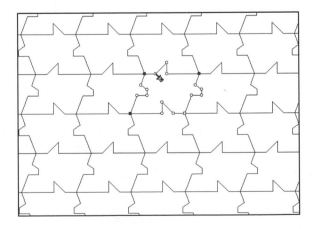

Show What You Have Learned

Describe any properties of the angles or sides of a quadrilateral that allow the quadrilateral to tessellate by a combination of glide reflection and translation.

Activity 12 • Glide Reflection and Midpoint Rotation

TesselMania!'s last transformation option combines glide reflection and midpoint rotation.

Open a new file and double-click on **Glide Reflection & Rotation.** You have three options—a triangle and two quadrilaterals. Since the triangle is selected by default, click on **Show Me** to see a modification to one side of the triangle flip about a reflection line and then slide to an adjacent side. Next a modification to half of the third side will rotate 180° about the midpoint of the side to the other half-side. Launch the triangle.

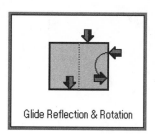

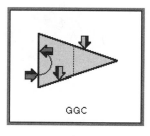

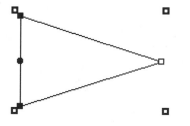

Activate the handles of the triangle, then deform it. Notice the restriction this transformation type imposes on the polygon. Two of its sides will always remain equal in length.

Open the file <triang02> in the <polygons> directory on the Explore disk. Modify the triangle with the **Tack,** but work around the angle labels. One side has a black circle at its midpoint. Any change to a half-side here results in a corresponding change to the other half-side. If you change one of the unmarked sides, the other unmarked side will also change. The triangle must be isosceles. Activate **Tile Magic,** and notice that the reflection line passes through the midpoints of the two equal sides.

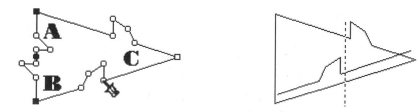

Examine the configuration of tiles in tessellation mode. Remember that a triangle's angles total 180°. Since two sets of the triangle's angles surround each vertex, there are 360° worth of angles around the vertex. Hence, there are no gaps, and the modified triangle tessellates.

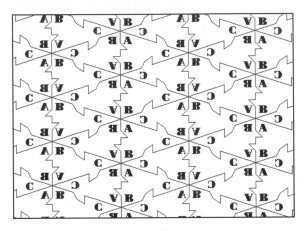

Open a new file and launch **Glide Reflection & Rotation.** This time, select either quadrilateral and then **Show Me.** *TesselMania!* makes a modification to one side of the tile, flips it, and slides it to another side—opposite it or adjacent to it. Then the program modifies each of two half-sides and rotates the change 180° about the midpoint of the side to its other half-side. Launch the quadrilateral on the left.

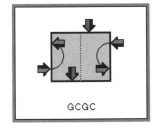

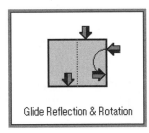

Activate the handles of the original square; then deform the tile as much as you can. You may conclude at first that any deformation is possible, but actually, two opposite sides of the quadrilateral will always remain equal to one another.

Open the file < quad09 >, and modify the tile with the **Tack**. When you change an unmarked side, a corresponding change appears on the opposite side, so their lengths must be equal. If you change a half-side, the related half-side will also change. Use **Tile Magic** to animate the creation of your modified tile. The reflection line passes through the center of the parent quadrilateral.

Select **Tessellation Magic** (in tessellation mode), and watch the four labeled angles of the original quadrilateral surround each vertex of the initial tile through a series of glide reflections and 180° rotations about the midpoints of sides. Since the sum of the angles in a quadrilateral is always 360°, any quadrilateral with a pair of equal opposite sides will tessellate by combining glide reflection and midpoint rotation.

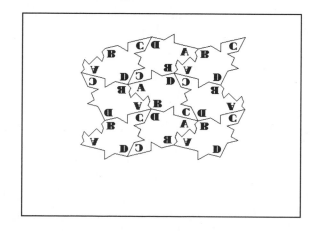

Stop the animation, open a new file, and again launch **Glide Reflection & Rotation.** This time, double-click on the quadrilateral on the right.

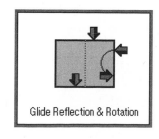

Glide Reflection & Rotation

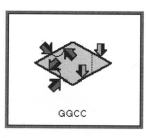

GGCC

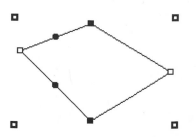

After activating the handles, try to deform this tile. It may look as though you can make any change you wish. However, two adjacent sides of the quadrilateral will always be equal to one another.

Open the file < quad10 >. As you modify an unmarked side of this quadrilateral, a corresponding change appears on the adjacent side rather than the opposite side. The lengths of these related sides are equal. As before, if you change a half-side, the related half-side will also change. **Tile Magic** will help you see how your changes create the new tile shape. Also, notice how the reflection line passes through the midpoints of the related equal sides.

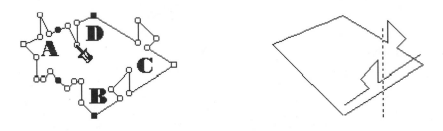

Select **Tessellation Magic** (in tessellation mode), and watch the four labeled angles of the quadrilateral surround each vertex of the initial tile through glide reflections, 180° rotations about the midpoints of sides, and translations (equivalent to two 180° rotations). Since the sum of the angles in a quadrilateral is always 360°, any quadrilateral with a pair of equal adjacent sides will tessellate by combining glide reflection and midpoint rotation. Stop the animation.

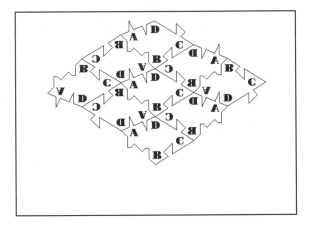

As a result of this activity, you can conclude that any triangle or quadrilateral with a pair of equal sides will tessellate by glide reflection and midpoint rotation.

Show What You Have Learned

Look at all six transformation types. Which transformation type gives you the most choices for a tile type? Which give the fewest choices? How many choices for tile type are there in all? How many transformation type choices are there for triangles? quadrilaterals? hexagons?

Activity 13 • Classifying Tiles

While doing earlier activities, you may have noticed the sequence of letters, such as TTTT and GCGC, beneath the various tile choices in the tile-picker screens. These labels come from a system for classifying tiles devised by German mathematician Heinrich Heesch. Heesch identified 28 different tile types. His system is based on how the transformations to the sides of a specific tile relate it to the tiles that surround it in a tessellation. His transformation types did not involve simple reflection.

The current version of *TesselMania!* includes 15 of the 28 tile types: 11 based on quadrilaterals, 2 based on triangles, and 2 based on hexagons. The available choices include all of Heesch's tile types based on quadrilaterals. (*TesselMania! Deluxe* includes all 28 of Heesch's tile types.)

Heesch's system provides a quick and easy way to identify tile types. The letters indicate the transformations or motions that relate the sides of the tile.

T = translation

C = 180° midpoint rotation

C_3 = 120° vertex rotation (three-fold center of rotation)

C_4 = 90° vertex rotation (four-fold center of rotation)

C_6 = 60° vertex rotation (six-fold center of rotation)

G = glide reflection

The number subscripts in vertex rotation indicate the fold of the vertex. If you multiply the fold and its angle of rotation, you always get 360°. The symbol C rather than C_2 is used for 180° midpoint rotation (two-fold center of rotation) to distinguish it from vertex rotation.

To get the Heesch type for a specific tile, start at the top of the tile and then move clockwise around its outline while assigning a letter label to each side. Since each side must be assigned a letter, the number of letters in the Heesch type is always the same as the number of sides of the parent polygon. Below are some other facts about Heesch's system.

- Sides changed by midpoint rotation are related to themselves. Other sides are related to an opposite side or to an adjacent side by a translation, rotation, or glide reflection.

- If you inspect the matching bumps and holes on the sides, you can discover the transformation type that was used. You may also lay tracing paper over a shape, trace a modified side; then slide, flip, or turn the paper to see how the related modified side was produced.

- For vertex rotation, you can estimate the angle of rotation. The angle will be either 120° (C_3), 90° (C_4), or 60° (C_6).

Look at the Heesch type for the tiles below. The tile TCTC shows translation and midpoint rotation. The other tile shows vertex rotation. The angle between the C_3 sides is 120°. The angle between the C_6 sides is 60°.

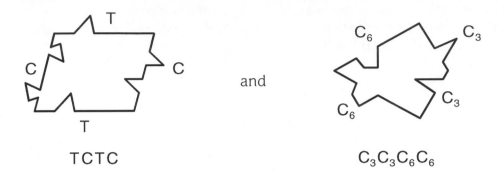

TCTC $C_3C_3C_6C_6$

If needed, use subscripts to show related sides. Because translations always occur between pairs of opposite sides, you don't need subscripts to distinguish between pairs of translations. Thus, TTTT tells you there is a translation between two pairs of opposite sides of a quadrilateral-based tile.

Glide reflections, on the other hand, can occur between pairs of opposite sides or between pairs of adjacent sides. If there is only one glide reflection, you don't need subscripts. For example, in GTGT, the glide reflection is between a pair of opposite sides of a quadrilateral-based tile. In CCGG, the glide occurs between a pair of adjacent sides.

If there is more than one glide reflection, use subscripts to show related sides. Thus, $G_1G_2G_1G_2$ tells you there are two glide reflections between pairs of opposite sides. $G_1G_1G_2G_2$ tells you there are two glide reflections between pairs of adjacent sides.

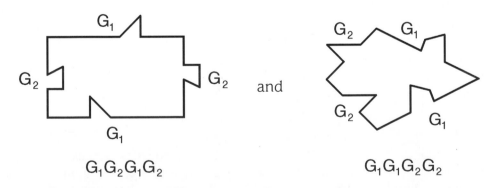

$G_1G_2G_1G_2$ $G_1G_1G_2G_2$

Even though Heesch's system isn't essential to understanding tessellating art, it will prove useful in later activities.

TesselMania! includes three on-screen pages of text about Heesch types. To read them, launch any transformation type and tile type; then select **Options: Heesch Type** (for Macintosh) or **Help: Heesch Type** (for Windows).

Show What You Have Learned

Write the corresponding Heesch type in the space beneath each of the following tiles. Three of the types cannot be created with *TesselMania!*.

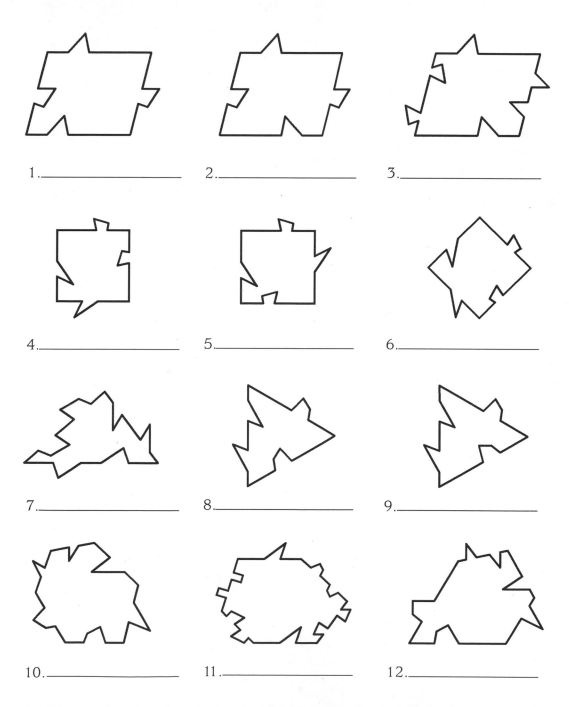

1._____   2._____   3._____

4._____   5._____   6._____

7._____   8._____   9._____

10._____   11._____   12._____

13. Choose one Heesch type not pictured, draw the tile, describe how you created it, and show how it will tessellate.

To the Teacher

Here are the answers for Activity 13.

1. TTTT
2. GTGT
3. GCGC
4. $C_4C_4C_4C_4$
5. $G_1G_2G_1G_2$
6. $G_1G_1G_2G_2$
7. CCC
8. GGC
9. C_6C_6C
10. $C_3C_3C_3C_3C_3C_3$
11. TCCTCC
12. $CC_3C_3C_6C_6$
13. Answers will vary.

Heesch's 28 tile types are listed below. They are pictured on page 326 of Doris Schattschneider's *Visions of Symmetry.* The cyclic order of the symbols is irrelevant. Those in italics cannot be implemented with the current version of *TesselMania!*.

Triangle Tiles

CCC	CC_3C_3	CC_6C_6
GGC	CC_4C_4	

Quadrilateral Tiles

TTTT	CCCC	$C_4C_4C_4C_4$	$G_1G_2G_1G_2$
TCTC	CCGG	$C_3C_3C_3C_3$	$G_1G_1G_2G_2$
GTGT	GCGC	$C_3C_3C_6C_6$	

Pentagonal Tiles

TCTCC	$CC_4C_4C_4C_4$	$CG_1G_2G_1G_2$
TCTGG	$CC_3C_3C_6C_6$	

Hexagonal Tiles

TTTTTT	$C_3C_3C_3C_3C_3C_3$	$TG_1G_2TG_2G_1$
TCCTCC	$CG_1CG_2G_1G_2$	$TG_1G_1TG_2G_2$
TCCTGG		

The existence of so many different types of tessellating pentagonal tiles is quite surprising even to those familiar with tessellations. Regular pentagons—with their angle measure of 108°—do not tessellate. Heesch's pentagonal tiles tessellate due to the specificity of their angle measures or their geometric outline as well as to the transformations used to generate the tessellation.

Chapter 2

Exploring *TesselMania!*'s Paint Tools

In the previous chapter, you explored the 15 types of tessellations *TesselMania!* can create, and you changed the outline of tiles using the **Arrow, Tack,** and **Scissors.** You discovered that the transformation type puts certain limits on how you could change the tile and yet still end up with a tile that tessellates.

TesselMania! also provides 13 paint tools for adding color and detail inside a tile. You can use these tools only in single-tile mode and only within the tile outline. In tessellation mode, the tools dim and you cannot select them.

The four activities in this chapter introduce the paint tools. They add to *TesselMania!*'s documentation by showing you how to modify the screen's *pixels,* the picture elements.

TesselMania!'s paint tools are similar to the tools found in other paint programs, such as *MacPaint* and *PC Paintbrush.* You can read short descriptions of *TesselMania!*'s paint tools in **Options: Instructions** (for Macintosh) or **Help: Instructions** (for Windows). You may also click on **Instructions** in the title screen.

These are the paint tools in *TesselMania!*.

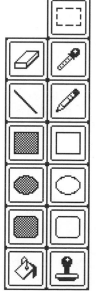

Use the MARQUEE to select an area to move, cut, copy, or delete.

Use the ERASER to erase part of the drawing.

Use the EYEDROPPER to select a color from the tile rather than the color palette.

Use the LINE to draw straight lines in the tile.

Use the PENCIL to add freehand drawing.

Use the FILLED SHAPES to add shapes filled with selected color and pattern.

Use the SHAPES to add shapes outlined in the selected color.

Use the PAINT BUCKET to fill an area with the selected color.

Use the STAMP to quickly add features and text to your tile.

Use the LINE WIDTH to select the width of the lines drawn with the Line, Pencil, and Shape tools.

Activity 14 • Color Pairs and Triplets

In this activity, you will learn to use color pairs and triplets, to select a color from a palette, to recall a color from a tile, and to rearrange the colors in a palette. You will also learn how to save a file to a disk or hard drive.

Open a new file by selecting **File: New,** double-click on **Translation,** and double-click on the quadrilateral [Heesch type TTTT].

A color palette appears directly beneath the window whenever you are working in single-tile mode.

Current Color   More Colors

The palette groups colors in pairs for all but two of *TesselMania!*'s quadrilateral types and for both of its triangle types. The pairs are contrasting colors, such as yellow and blue. Notice the frame around the top box of the pair of black boxes (double-black) at the extreme right end (for Macintosh) or extreme left end (for Windows) of the palette. The selected color also appears in the large box to the left of the palette.

To select a different color, simply click on it. Click on the yellow of the yellow/blue pair. The frame moves and the color of the large box changes accordingly. To view more colors, click on the arrow buttons to the right of the

palette.

Select the **Paint Bucket;** then move the cursor into the tile. The cursor now looks like a bucket of paint. Rest the tip of the dripping paint on the area you wish to color—in this case, the

entire tile. If you click the mouse button, yellow paint spills to fill the tile.

Select a different color in the pallete. The large box to the left of the palette changes to that color. If you now wish to return to yellow, you can use the **Eyedropper** to recall it without returning to the color palette. After selecting the **Eyedropper,** position the tip of its cursor over the yellow color in the tile; then click.

Yellow is automatically selected on the color palette. The former color is the current color again.

Now select **Tessellate,** and watch the tessellation fill the window. *TesselMania!* paints adjacent tiles in contrasting colors to distinguish them from one another. Whenever you paint or draw with one color, the contrasting color appears in the adjacent tile automatically. However, if you want all tiles to be colored the same, select **Tile: Same Colors.** Select **Tile: Contrasting Colors** to return to two colors. A check always appears next to the current option.

Open a new file. This time double-click on **Translation** and on the hexagon [Heesch type TTTTT].

The color palette for hexagons (and for Heesch types $C_3C_3C_3C_3$ and $C_3C_3C_6C_6$) groups colors in triplets instead of pairs.

Paint your hexagon any color using the **Paint Bucket;** then select **Tessellate.** The color triplets appear in adjacent tiles automatically. Use **Tile: Same Colors** to see all tiles colored the same. Return to **Contrasting Colors.**

You are not limited to the color pairs and triplets *TesselMania!* first offers. Select **Options: Edit Colors.** This opens a dialog box. Click on any of the colors in your triplet, one of which will be framed; then drag the cursor to a new position. When you release the mouse button, the new color and the old color swap places. Only the multiple-black and multiple-white boxes at the ends of the palettes cannot be moved.

Select **OK** to return to the window, and see the effect on your tessellation. You may also edit colors, but since the procedure differs for Macintosh and Windows users, read your software documentation on how to do this. The documentation will also tell you how to load color palettes from other files.

Select **File: Save As.** Give your file a name, and save it to disk or hard drive. As with other software, you can use the **Save** command when you edit the file later. *TesselMania!* saves any changes you make to the palette with your file.

If you wish to give yourself credit, select **Options: Footer.** This opens a dialog box in which you can enter text. When you click **Use Footer** (for Macintosh) or **Show Footer** (for Windows), your credit will appear at the bottom of the screen in tessellation mode. It will also appear at the bottom of the printout when you print the tessellation.

Return to single-tile mode; then modify the outline of the colored hexagon with the **Tack.** You will have to patch color into the new bumps you create. The hidden, former color of new holes may even bleed into adjacent tiles. Consequently, you should add color and detail only after you've finished modifying the tile's outline.

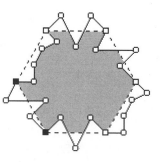

Show What You Have Learned

Show how to use the **Paint Bucket** and the **Eyedropper.** Create a new color palette for a tile type that uses color pairs; then create one for a tile type that uses color triplets.

Activity 15 • Classic Drawing Tools

In this activity, you will learn to use *TesselMania!*'s tools—the **Line,** the **Pencil,** and the Filled Shape—for drawing on (or adding markings to) the interior of a tile. The **Eraser** will be introduced as well.

Open a new file, double-click on **Translation,** and then on the quadrilateral [Heesch type TTTT].

Select the **Line.** This tool draws straight lines in the selected color and line width. Move the cursor into the tile until the intersection of its cross-hair markings touches the point where you want the line to begin. Drag the cursor in any direction until the line is as long as you want it; then release the mouse button. Unless you change the settings, you will get a black line in the thinnest line width.

The **Line Width** box tells you the selected width with arrows (for Macintosh) or with a frame (for Windows). Click on the second line width, then draw another line within the tile. This width is good for contrast. Add two more lines to your tile using the third and fourth line widths—you'll probably only use these widths occasionally.

Back in tessellation mode, select or activate **Tile: Invert Black/White** for an interesting effect. Turn off the option when you are done.

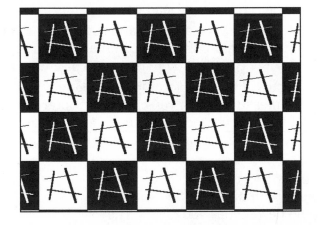

Return to single-tile mode. Add several colored lines; then color the background regions of the tile in a different color with the **Paint Bucket.** Select **Tessellate.** Adjacent tiles appear in contrasting colors. Discover the effect of **Tile: Invert Black/White** and **Tile: Same Colors.** Turn off **Invert Black/White,** and return to **Tile: Contrasting Colors** when you are done.

Return to single-tile mode. Select **Edit: Erase Painting** to erase all painting and detail inside the tile.

You can use the **Shape** tools (**Rectangle, Oval,** and **Rounded Rectangle**) to draw shapes outlined in the current color and the corresponding **Filled Shape** tools to draw shapes filled with the current color or pattern.

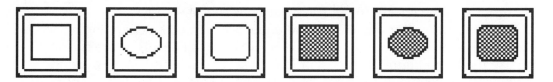

Select any of these tools, move the cursor into the tile, drag the cursor to produce the shape or filled shape; then release the mouse button. The figure will be drawn from the corner in the color, pattern, and line width you selected. As you may have learned with the **Line** tool, *TesselMania!* cuts off any portion extending beyond the edge of the tile.

If you hold down the shift key and drag the cursor, you can restrict a rectangle to a square, an oval to a circle, and a rounded rectangle to a rounded square. (Regrettably, the Windows version of the software does not draw perfectly symmetrical ovals or circles.)

Select **Edit: Erase Painting** again so you can experiment with the **Shape** and **Filled Shape** tools. Vary the colors and line widths. Try coloring both shapes and filled shapes with the **Paint Bucket.**

Erase the painting again, and create an abstract or geometrical design with the **Line** and **Shape** tools. Try to recreate the Islamic art grid at the right. Use **Edit: Undo** to quickly clear mistakes.

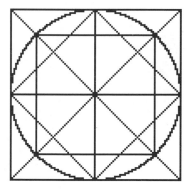

Color the various regions of your design with the **Paint Bucket;** then tessellate your tile. How does it look using **Same Colors** as compared to **Contrasting Colors?** If you wish, save your artwork. Return to single-tile mode, and erase your painting.

TesselMania! does not have a curved-line tool, but it does have a **Pencil.** You can use this tool like a regular pencil to add freehand drawing inside a tile. You can select the line's color and width. Click on the **Pencil,** and put the tip of the cursor where you wish to begin drawing. Drag the cursor as you draw a freehand curve. When you are done, release the mouse button.

Practice freehand drawing in a variety of colors and line widths. It is hard to draw accurately with the **Pencil.** Activity 16 will show you how to fine-tune your drawings.

Select the **Eraser.** This tool lets you eliminate specific color or detail inside a tile. It will not erase the tile border. Inside the tile, the eraser wipes out whatever is beneath it when you click the mouse button. If you drag the cursor, the eraser wipes out whatever passes beneath it until you release the mouse button.

Use the **Eraser** to eliminate a portion of your drawing. The operation will be very crude. When you want to erase, color, or add small details or areas, you can use the zoom buttons on the command bar to get a close-up view before you begin. The four zoom buttons—**1X, 2X, 4X,** and **8X**—provide a 100%, 200%, 400%, and 800% close-up view of a tile, respectively.

Examine your drawing at the various levels of magnification by clicking on the buttons. At **4X** and **8X,** your tile becomes larger than the window. Select the **Hand** tool (formerly the **Arrow** at **1X** or normal magnification), move to the window; then drag the cursor until you slide the desired portion of the drawing into view. Try erasing at the various levels.

You can use each of the drawing tools at all four levels of magnification. Erase your painting; then experiment with the tools in the various zoom modes. Your drawings will appear jagged at high magnification because every marking actually consists of a group of rectangles.

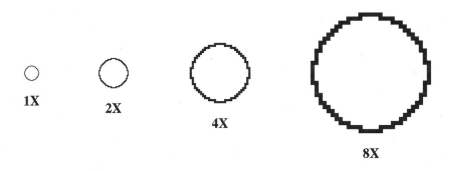

Show What You Have Learned

Show how to use the **Line, Pencil, Eraser,** and the various **Shape** and **Filled Shape** tools in *TesselMania!*'s toolbox using a variety of line widths, colors, and zoom modes.

Activity 16 • Pixel Perfect

In this activity, you will learn to do fine-tune editing to your drawings.

Open a new file. Double-click on **Translation** and the quadrilateral [Heesch type TTTT]. Zoom to **8X** magnification. Select the **Pencil** with the thinnest line width. Click the mouse button once in the window. A square dot or pixel appears.

The inside of your TTTT tile has almost 10,000 pixel locations. Line widths vary from one pixel to four. *TesselMania!* automatically makes tile borders one pixel wide for Windows users and two pixels wide for Macintosh users. You can change the width of the border by selecting **Tile: Tile Border.**

Pixels act like light bulbs—white when they are off and black or colored when they are on. If Macintosh users click on the same pixel again with the **Pencil,** it will turn white. Windows users must select the double-white color and click on the pixel with the **Pencil.** To change a single pixel to a color other than white, select the color, and click on the pixel with the **Pencil.**

Pixels are ordinarily unrelated or independent. When you draw with a tool, you turn on a group of pixels in the current color. If you use the paint bucket on a pixel, you affect all adjoining pixels of the same color.

If your drawing has a gap in what appears to be an enclosed region, paint will spill out into the next region. If this happens, select **Undo,** scan the region in a zoom mode until you find the gap, patch it with the **Pencil,** and begin again. Sometimes a pixel that is part of a region will not be colored because it shares only a corner with the region. The color flaws will stand out. Simply patch the color of each flawed pixel with the **Pencil** in a zoom mode. Remember you can recall a color with the **Eyedropper.**

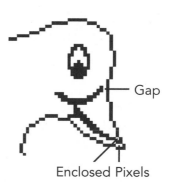

Gap

Enclosed Pixels

With any drawing tool, once you release the mouse button, all affected pixels become independent once again. You then deal with them pixel by pixel. To change the color of a line or shape, you need to change the color of all of its pixels with the **Pencil, Line,** or **Paint Bucket.** This may require a zoom mode and several clicks of the mouse if the pixels do not share an edge.

The **Eraser** will turn off all pixels that contact its cursor. However, even in zoom mode, it is too large to eliminate individual enclosed pixels. Instead, use the **Pencil** like a single-pixel eraser.

Show What You Have Learned

Open any of the files in the directory < pixel > on the Explore disk. Edit the detail in the tile with the **Pencil.** Use the **Paint Bucket** to color enclosed regions. Practice editing the problem pixels.

Activity 17   •   Other Tools

In this activity, you will learn to use the rest of the tools in *TesselMania!*'s toolbox, to use a pattern palette, and to use the editing commands.

Open a new file, launch **Translation** and the quadrilateral [Heesch type TTTT]. The pattern palette is below the color palette. It appears whenever you are working in single-tile mode and are using any tool except the **Stamp.** Notice the frame around the solid pattern. The current pattern in the current color (solid black by default) appears in the large box to the left of the palette. To view more patterns, click on the arrow buttons to the right of the palette.

Select a blue color in the color palette and the ninth pattern from the left in the pattern palette (the large dots). The frames will move accordingly. Blue appears in the large box to the left of the color palette. Large, blue dots appear in the box to the left of the pattern palette.

Select the **Paint Bucket;** then color the tile. It fills with blue dots on a white background. Suppose you want blue dots on a red background: Select a red color and the solid pattern from your palettes. Zoom in; then touch the drip of the **Paint Bucket** to any white pixel within the pattern. Because all the white pixels join together, the background turns red! (If you color the tile solid red before you add the pattern of blue dots, you will get blue dots on a white background.) With more refined patterns, you may end up with several enclosed regions to color. The background of the pattern may require pixel-by-pixel coloring. You can even edit the patterns themselves pixel by pixel.

Return to normal magnification. Select **Edit: Erase Painting,** color the tile a solid red with the **Paint Bucket;** then draw a filled oval anywhere on the tile using the pattern of blue dots. The Macintosh program draws an oval outlined in the current line width and filled with the pattern. The Windows program draws an oval in the pattern with no border. Try coloring the background of the pattern in another solid color. Keep experimenting so you can master using the patterns.

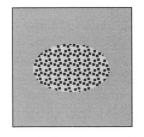

Erase your painting again and get ready to use a really fun tool—a picture stamper!

Select the **Stamp**. This tool imprints features, objects, letters, and numbers in a tile. Like regular stamps, *TesselMania!*'s stamps have a predetermined shape and size. They will print in a selected color over white, black, or colored backgrounds. However, enclosed pixels within the stamp outline will be white.

When you select the **Stamp,** stamp icons replace the patterns across the bottom of the screen. To view more icons, click on the arrow buttons to the right of the palette. *TesselMania!* has two sizes of each stamp. Click on the **1X** button for the original size or **2X** for double size.

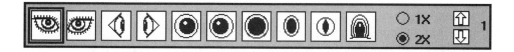

Click on the strawberry stamp icon from the ninth set of stamps. Select the red of a red/green pair on the color palette. Everyone likes big strawberries, so select **2X** or double size.

As you enter the tile, the cursor turns into a big, red strawberry. Place the stamp in a corner of the tile, then click the mouse button. Notice that the stamp is still active. It stays active until you select another tool or command. Add another strawberry, then select **Tessellate**. Tasty, but the tile needs sprucing up!

Just like pattern imprints, stamp imprints consist of pixels and can be edited. Go back to single-tile mode. Try coloring all the red pixels on the screen in double-black with the **Paint Bucket** or **Pencil**. Zoom in to get a close-up view. Of course, you could simply stamp on top of the imprint in double-black. Try adding and removing strawberry seeds with the **Pencil** in the thinnest line width. Use the **Paint Bucket** to color the inside of each strawberry red and the background of the tile green using the same red/green pair. Select **Tessellate** for a more interesting result. It just takes a little imagination!

This activity concludes with another of *TesselMania!*'s drawing tools—the **Marquee.** This tool lets you select a rectangular area within a tile outline. It is the most versatile and useful of the software's tools—particularly for Macintosh users.

Return to single-tile mode, and erase the painting. Draw a small oval within the tile using the **Oval;** then select the **Marquee.** Move the cursor until the intersection of its cross-hair markings lie just outside the rectangular boundary of the oval. Drag the cursor over the oval; then release the mouse button. The region within the moving dash lines has been selected. If you move the cursor inside the selection, it changes into a hand you can use to drag the selection anywhere within the tile. The selection remains active until you click outside it.

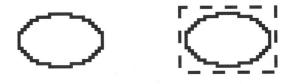

Erase your painting and draw another oval. This time, color the background of the tile with the **Paint Bucket.** Draw another marquee around the oval. If you drag the selection, you will find that all pixels in the rectangle are selected.

A good rule of thumb is to make the enveloping rectangle as small as possible. You may need to use a zoom mode with the **Marquee.** In the Windows program, you deactivate any selection whenever you change the level of magnification. That is another reason to always draw first and color last.

You can also use an active selection with any of the classic commands in the **Edit** menu (**Cut, Copy,** and **Paste**).

If you copy a group of pixels from a current or saved *TesselMania!* file, you can paste the selection into the current, a new, or a saved *TesselMania!* file if the selection is not bigger than the place you want to put it.

TesselMania! pastes the active selection in the center of the tile, but you can move it. This is useful if you wish to create or edit a group of pixels in one file before you select, copy, and paste the group into the tile of another file.

In the Windows *TesselMania!,* the **Copy** command copies an entire tile in tile mode when you use it without making a marquee selection. The Macintosh version copies the entire window in tile or tessellation mode. Macintosh users can use the **Copy** and **Paste** commands to export or import selections into or from other Macintosh programs.

Show What You Have Learned

Fill a square tile with a pattern on a colored background. Add an imprint of your name or initials with the **Stamp.** You may need to patch the background of the individual letters. Use the **Marquee** to copy and paste the contents of the tile into a larger hexagonal tile. Then, save your result.

Chapter 3

Creating Tessellating Art

To many users, *TesselMania!* is merely a toy. These users pick a transformation and tile type, pull out or in a few tacks at random, color the abstract shape, and stamp in eyes and a few other features. They tessellate the tile into their artistic masterpiece; then they repeat the process until they get bored.

The following pages will help you tackle unusual explorations and create interesting tessellations. In this chapter, you will construct a tessellating shape with a recognizable outline. In the next chapter, you will learn how to reconstruct or reverse engineer existing samples of tessellating art—including the tessellations of M. C. Escher. In the last two chapters, you will explore the creation of quilt patterns and Islamic art designs.

To help you along, the text will lead you step-by-step through constructing a tile with a recognizable outline and with interior details. Since profiles are easier to draw and to recognize, the next activity develops a tessellating profile.

Be sure to read Chapters 1 and 2 before doing the following activities, even if you have used paint programs before. You will especially need the pixel-editing training from Activity 16.

After you have completed the activities in this chapter, start creating your own tessellating art. Explore all 15 of *TesselMania!*'s transformation and tile types (or all 28 types in *TesselMania! Deluxe*). Take the time to produce recognizable outlines. You can begin with a specific object in mind or experiment with an outline until it begins to resemble an object. There are no steadfast rules. Try using all of the tools in the toolbox. Above all, use your imagination!

Activity 18 • A Step-by-Step Construction

Now that you have learned about tessellating shapes and have mastered the tools in *TesselMania!*'s toolbox, you are ready to create genuine tessellating art. In this activity, you will construct a pirate's head. How you proceed is up to you—these steps are just a suggestion.

Step 1. Open a new file by selecting **File: New,** double-click on **Translation;** then double-click on the quadrilateral [Heesch type TTTT].

Step 2. Change the tile's border. You can easily create a face outline using the **Tack**. Pull out a nose and pull in a mouth cavity as shown below on the left. By adding just two more tack points, you can create a crown for the head and the outline of a protruding bandanna (or hair, if you prefer) as shown below on the right. Adjust your tack points—or add additional ones—until you have a recognizable outline.

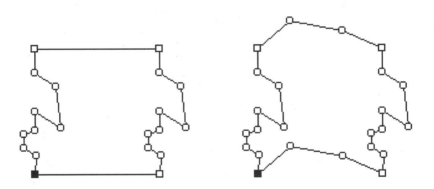

Step 3. Now add some details with the various drawing tools. For best contrast, use double-black and the two-pixel line width. At any time, Windows users can change the border to two pixels (second option), the default width for Macintosh users, by using **Tile: Tile Border.** Be aware that this slows down the speed of the program in any of the magic modes. Create the interior outline of the bandanna (or hair) with the **Line** tool.

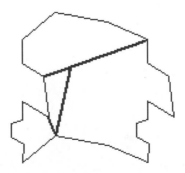

Step 4. Add an eye, a mouth, and an ear with the **Stamp** tool. You could also imprint these features in any color or create them with any of *TesselMania!*'s drawing tools. Add a circular earring below the pirate's ear by holding down the shift key as you use the **Oval** tool.

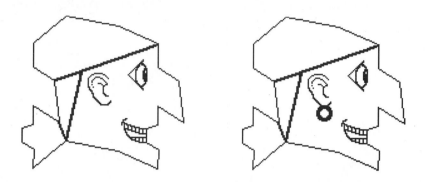

Step 5. Zoom in and add further detail. For example, pour black paint into a few of the pirate's teeth, or add random beard stubble pixel by pixel with the pencil in the thinnest line width. You could also use the **Pencil** or **Line** to draw a scar on the pirate's cheek.

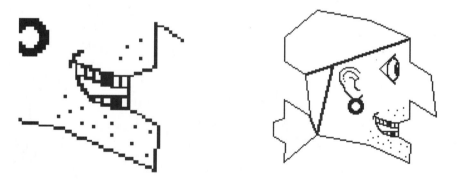

Step 6. If all of your details are double-black, select **Tessellate** and activate **Tile: Invert Black/White** to see an interesting effect. Turn off the option when you are done.

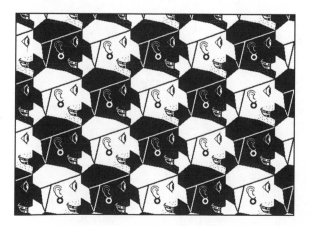

Step 7. Return to single-tile mode; then color the regions of your tile with the **Paint Bucket.** You may want to change the color pair combinations using **Options: Edit Colors.** Zoom in to patch the color of any enclosed pixels with the **Pencil** in the thinnest line width. Use the **Eyedropper** to recall any color. Select **Tessellate.** Adjacent tiles appear in contrasting colors unless you change the selection in the **Tile** menu.

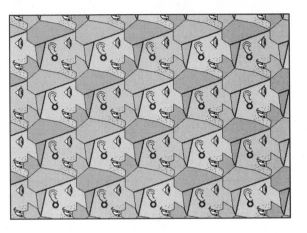

Step 8. Select **Options: Footer;** then give yourself credit. Don't forget to click on **Use Footer** (for Macintosh) or **Show Footer** (for Windows). Save your completed drawing to a disk or hard drive. To see one completed pirate, open < pirate > in the directory < tessart > .

Step 9. If you wish, explore the various magic options. Try activating the **Invert Black/White** option to see the effect. Or, compare the effect of the **Same Colors** and **Contrasting Colors** options.

Select **Options: Show Grid.** Notice how more than two tessellating shapes meet at each vertex of the parent squares. Turn off **Show Grid** when you are done.

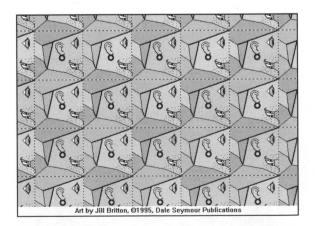

Art by Jill Britton, ©1995, Dale Seymour Publications

Show What You Have Learned.

Create your own tessellating art. Use a variety of transformation and tile types, tools, and palettes. Present your artwork in the various magic modes.

Activity 19 • A Tessellation Slide Show

A convenient way to view your tessellating art is in a slide show.

Select **File: Slide Show.** The dialog box allows you to select a *TesselMania!* file from anywhere on disk or hard drive. Select a file of your choice. For example, select the file < pirate > in the directory < tessart > on the Explore disk. The slide show begins with the selected file, followed by the other files in the directory. The order depends upon the version of the software.

In slide-show mode, the file names appear at the top of the screen. Footer information appears at the bottom (if you saved the file with the option selected).

The slider bar controls the speed of the display, and three buttons control its direction. You can pause or renew the show at any time by clicking on the **Pause** button. To quit, click on **Stop.**

For a creative slide show, save your drawing at each stage of construction numbering the files in sequence. Put the files in order in one directory and open the first file in slide show mode.

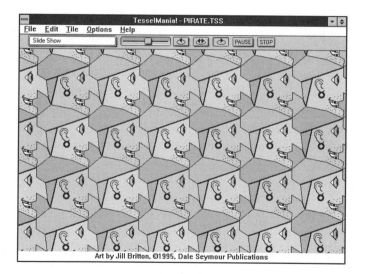

The Explore disk has two directories of tessellating art files: < tessart > and < reverse >. The files have been classified by Heesch type in the table on page 54. In the next chapter, you will use several of these files. You can preview them now in a slide show.

Open several of the files in the directory < tessart >, selecting **Options: Show Grid** each time. You will find that more than two tessellating shapes meet at each vertex of the parent polygons. You will use this fact when you attempt to reconstruct a piece of tessellating art in the next chapter.

Show What You Have Learned

Use the slide-show feature to explore the files in the various directories of the Explore disk and in the examples directory of the *TesselMania!* disk.

Tessellating Art on Disk

TYPE	HEESH-TYPE	TESSART Macintosh	TESSART Windows	REVERSE
Translation	TTTT	pirate dogear bird-on-bull	pirate dogear birdbull	elephant
	TTTTTT	mice woodpecker creature	mice woodpeck creature	hockey
Rotation	CCC	frog whale	frog whale	birdisos
	CCCC	coyote spectre	coyote spectre	dogquad laughdog parrot
	$C_4C_4C_4C_4$	bunny stuble	bunny stuble	birdsqua moose
	$C_3C_3C_3C_3$	sheep mushrooms	sheep dancer	clown
	$C_3C_3C_6C_6$	doggy mermaids	doggy sealhead	
	$C_3C_3C_3C_3C_3C_3$	mouse prince	mouse prince	birdhex
Glide Reflection	$G_1G_2G_1G_2$	bear mallard	bear mallard	bug
	$G_1G_1G_2G_2$	eagle	eagle	seal escher67
Translation & Rotation	TCTC	fish storyteller	fish ballgirl	rabbit dogtie escher75
Glide Reflection & Translation	GTGT	like cool train	likecool train	goldfish
Glide Reflection & Rotation	GGC	vulture	vulture	bluebird
	GCGC	dove animals	dove camile	
	GGCC	pharaoh chicken	pharaoh chicken	

© Del ... ... Publications ®

Chapter 4

Reverse-Engineering

In this chapter, you will use *TesselMania!* to reverse-engineer a sample of tessellating art. Reverse-engineering is the process of analyzing an object to discover the details of its design in order to reconstruct it. You could compare it to the problem-solving strategy of working backward. This reconstruction process is not precise, but the results can be quite striking.

You will find blackline drawings of six tessellations in this chapter. All were created using an expensive computer-draw program. When you magnify these computer images, you see smooth curves—not pixels. You can reconstruct all of them with *TesselMania!*. In fact, you will find a sample reconstruction of each in the directory < reverse > on the Explore disk. Their filenames are < rabbit >, < elephant >, < parrot >, < goldfish >, < bluebird >, and < clown >.

In the directory, you will find other examples of tessellating art created by reverse-engineering. All files have been classified according to Heesch type in the table on page 54. You can find the original line drawings in *Introduction to Tessellations* and *Teaching Tessellating Art,* both available from Dale Seymour Publications.

The master creator of tessellating shapes was Dutch graphic artist M. C. Escher (1898–1972). You will find two of Escher's tessellations at the end of this chapter and another two on pages 75 and 76 of the *TesselMania!* documentation. A multimedia journey through Escher's life and work including an art gallery with hundreds of prints and drawings is available on the CD-ROM *Escher Interactive.*

Escher's tessellations are famous for having easy-to-identify outlines. His added details simply confirm the interpretation. Escher printed the original tessellations in black or colored ink using a woodcut block or by lithography. The book *Visions of Symmetry* by Doris Schattschneider is a good source of reproductions of Escher's tessellation (see the bibliography).

As you try to reconstruct Escher's work with *TesselMania!,* you will gain a hands-on appreciation of the artist's genius. You will also discover which of Escher's tessellations cannot be reconstructed with the current version of the software. (Some of these can be reconstructed with *TesselMania! Deluxe.*)

A reconstruction of Escher Print 75 and the interlocking shapes of Print 67 (his famous horseman) appear with permission in the directory < reverse >. Any reconstruction is only a suggestion of the original. It is not a true reproduction. A reproduction of Print 75 appears on page 66.

Remember you can use **File: Slide Show** to preview the tessellations in any directory. You can also open each file and analyze the tessellations using the magic options. Using **Options: Show Grid** will also be helpful in analyzing the tessellations.

Activity 20 • Reconstructing Tessellating Art

In this activity, you will learn a procedure for reconstructing or reverse-engineering a sample of tessellating art with *TesselMania!*.

Step 1. Select a graphic whose tessellating shape is not bigger than 2.5 inches in height or in width. If you have an unusual monitor or graphic, reduce or enlarge the drawing as needed. For your first effort, pick a shape with a simple contour and design. The rascally rabbit below makes an excellent choice.

Step 2. To find the parent polygon, go completely around an enclosed tessellating shape with your finger. Look for all points where more than two shapes meet. Four rabbits meet at the each of the dots shown below. Connect these dots as you go around the shape again and you'll see that the rabbit tessellation is based on a rectangle.

Step 3. Use a piece of clear acetate and a fine, colored marker to trace the shape. Also trace the details and the parent polygon. Study the transformations. It looks as though the rabbit has Heesch type TCTC.

The quadrilateral was modified by translation to one pair of parallel sides and by rotation about the midpoints of the other sides.

Step 4. Open a new file, and launch the appropriate transformation and tile type. In the case of the rabbit, you choose the pair of transformations **Translation & Rotation** followed by TCTC—the only choice.

Step 5. The program determines the transformation that will be used between particular sides or half-sides of your tile. This cannot be altered. Test each side with the **Tack** to discover how it will be changed. Tape your tracing to the computer screen so the orientation of sides and half-sides using specific transformations agrees with that of your screen tile. Activate the handles of the tile; then move its corners with the **Arrow** until they match the corners of the parent rectangle on your tracing. Macintosh users may wish to reset **Tile: Tile Border** to one pixel.

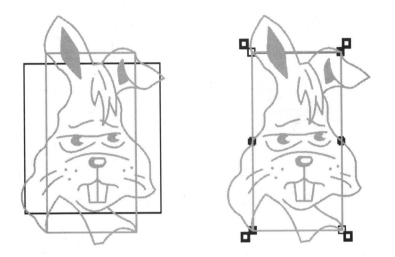

Step 6. Now change the outline of the tile with the **Tack** until it matches your tracing. If *TesselMania!* doesn't allow you a move—for example, when one modification crosses another—first modify another section; then return when the outline is more complete. Use **Options: Show Grid** if you wish to see the parent polygon in the background.

Step 7. Select **Tessellate.** Since the acetate makes it hard to see the border of the original tile, adjust the tack points in tessellation mode until the border of the other tiles appears smooth. Add additional points if you need to.

Step 8. Return to single-tile mode to add the features. Double-black in the thinnest line width works well. You may trace some features with the **Oval** and delete any excess with the **Eraser** in a zoom mode. Most features can be created with short spurts of the **Line** tool. Zoom in and edit the pixels with the **Pencil.** Macintosh users can turn pixels on and off. Windows users must color them black or white.

Step 9. Color the tile with the **Paint Bucket,** taking care to patch any enclosed pixels with the **Pencil.** You may also select **Tile: Invert Black/White** for an Escher-like effect. Tessellate your tile; then save your artwork.

A colored sample of the rabbit tessellation appears in < rabbit > in the directory < reverse > on the Explore disk. You will also find another interpretation of the shape under the filename < dogtie > .

Show What You Have Learned

Reconstruct a sample of tessellating art, editing the pixels as needed. Color the tessellating tile, taking care to patch any enclosed pixels—then tessellate!

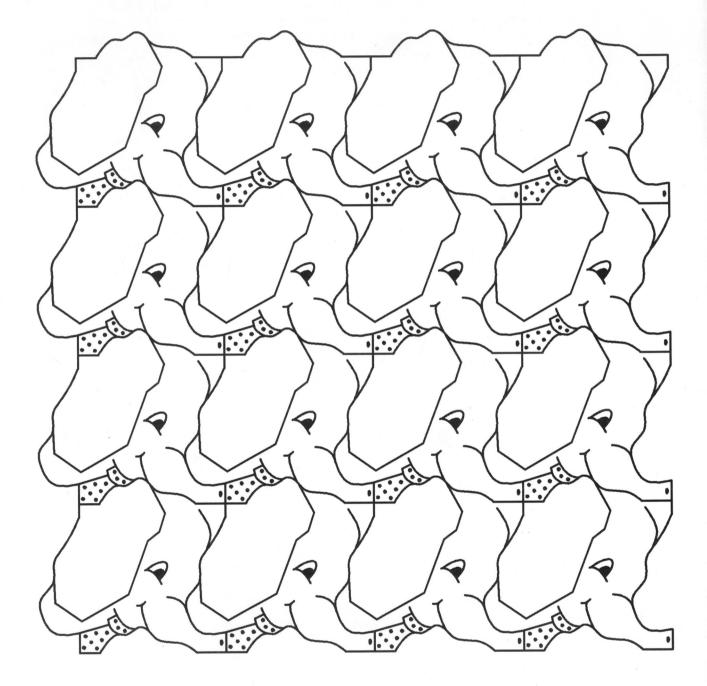

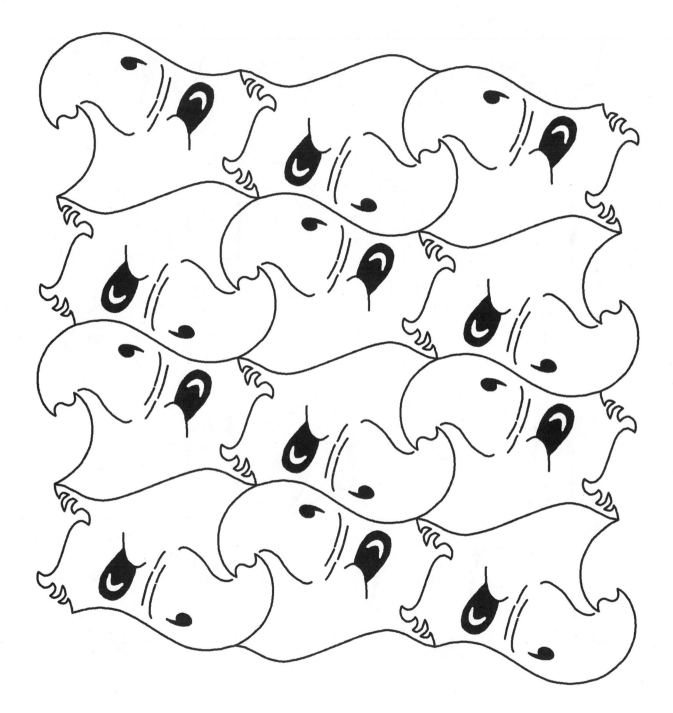

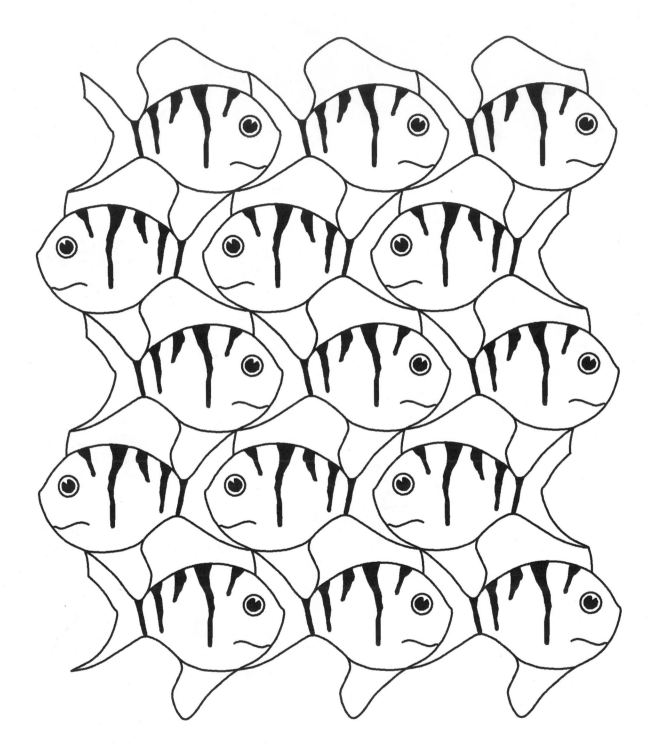

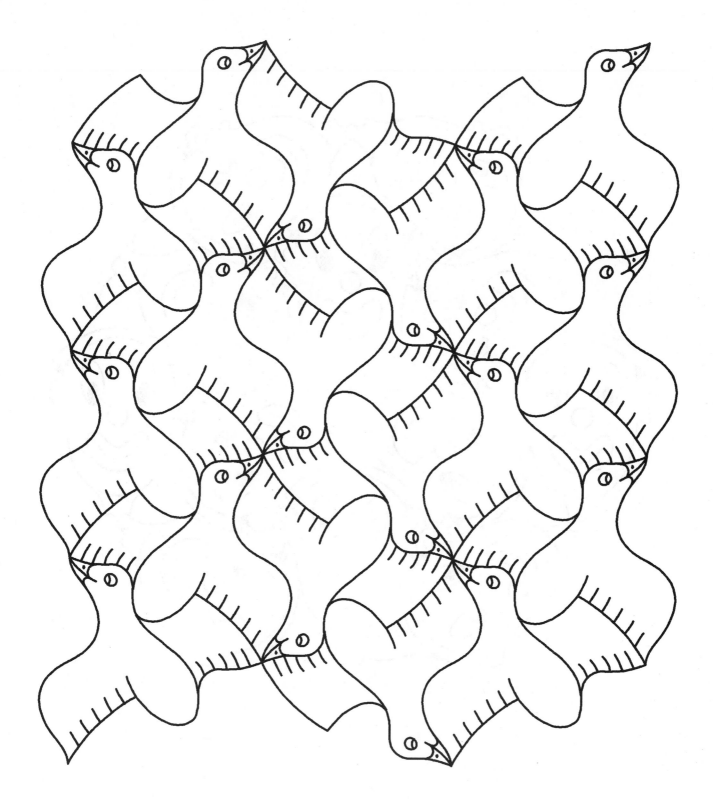

M. C. Escher Print 104

M. C. Escher Print 75

Explorations with *TesselMania!*

Chapter 5

TesselMania! and Quilt Design

Every quilter dreams of browsing through an attic and discovering a perfectly stitched and beautifully preserved patchwork quilt. Quilts are cherished for their creative patterns as well as for their detailed handiwork.

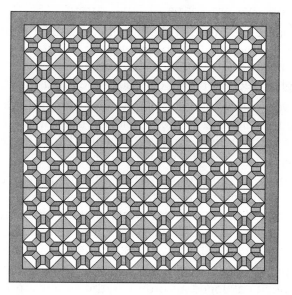

The basic unit of each patchwork pattern is the block—this design element repeats throughout the quilt top. Each block is made up of individual pieces of cloth called *patches*.

Most traditional American patchwork quilts are constructed from identical square blocks that are joined to make a continuous cloth tessellation. The range of block patterns is phenomenal—from very simple patterns to very complex ones.

In this chapter, you will learn how to recreate these traditional patterns. You will also be able to create new ones.

Since *TesselMania!* does not have any ruler guides, using the software to recreate a quilt block might seem impossible. Fortunately, the square blocks of most traditional patchwork quilts are made up of rectangles, parallelograms, trapezoids, and other simple polygons. You can subdivide these shapes into just squares and right isosceles triangles by superimposing a grid of squares.

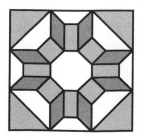

Prosperity Block

(Nine-by-Nine grid)

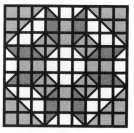

Here's what you could do to make a tessellating quilt block. First, select a transformation and tile type in *TesselMania!* that is suitable for a square, for example, Heesch type TTTT. Subdivide the square tile into a grid of identical, smaller squares. Add the necessary diagonals; then eliminate all horizontal and vertical line segments that are not part of the pattern.

Subdividing a square tile into a grid of identical, smaller squares (for example, three by three, four by four, and so on) involves carefully counting pixels between the horizontal and vertical lines. Depending on how many subdivisions you want, you might need to enlarge or reduce the tile using its handles.

This is a lot of work, so to help you along, nine standard grids have already been drawn for you within a TTTT tile. You'll find them in the directory < sqgrids > on the Explore disk. Activity 21 will lead you through a step-by-step procedure to create a quilt out of one of these grids.

Rather than produce a complete set of nine standard grids for each Heesch type, you can use a TTTT grid to draw the quilt block. You can then copy and paste the result—colored or not—into another Heesch type. Activity 22 teaches you how to do this. The activity uses vertex rotation [Heesch type $C_4C_4C_4C_4$], but you can adapt the method for any Heesch type that is suitable for a square.

A library of traditional quilt-block patterns appears on pages 74 to 81. Each block pattern has been cataloged according to the simplest grid required to subdivide it into just squares and right isosceles triangles. The blocks have been named—although there are lots of different names for many patterns. The blank grids on page 82 are for you to practice designing your own quilt blocks. You can learn more about quilt blocks in *Quilt Design Masters* by Luanne Seymour Cohen (see the bibliography).

Activity 23 explores the importance of color and pattern in the patches of a quilt block. The directory < quilts# > contains uncolored quilt blocks, and < quilts > contains ideas for coloring the quilts. The cover of *Quilt Design Masters* and the companion poster, *Patterns Within Patterns,* displays nine variations of the Old Maid's Puzzle. They look very different not only because of the colors but also because of the transformations used to combine blocks.

Once you begin exploring with pattern and color, you will find it difficult to decide which designs you like best.

Activity 21 • Creating a Quiltlike Tessellation

The following steps allow you to reproduce any of the traditional quilt blocks shown on pages 74 to 81 as a *TesselMania!* tile. Once you master the process, design your own patterns in the blank grids on page 82 and then recreate them with the software. You don't have to be artistically gifted to be creative with quilt blocks—just careful!

Step 1. Select a quilt-block pattern from the illustrations on pages 74 to 81. For this example, choose the four-by-four block called Cube Lattice (quilt 15).

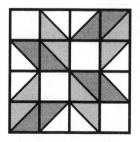

Step 2. Create a transparency of the page of blank square grids (page 82). Or trace the appropriate grid onto clear acetate with a fine, colored marker. Cube Lattice uses a four-by-four grid, so align the transparent four-by-four grid over the Cube Lattice block and tape it in place. Notice the diagonal lines on the block. They extend from corner to corner on the grid squares.

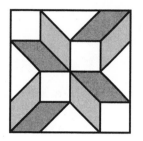

Step 3. Open the directory <sqgrids> on the Explore disk. Select the file you need. For Cube Lattice, open the file <4x4>. Select **2X** to enlarge the view.

Step 4. Using the **Line** in double-black and the thinnest line width, add all appropriate diagonal lines to the grid on the screen. Both cross hairs of the cursor should line up with the horizontal and vertical grid lines when you push the mouse button to begin a diagonal line and again when you release it. Where possible, both cross hairs will turn white or be framed in white when positioned correctly. Each diagonal line should have exactly one pixel per row and column.

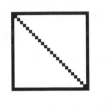 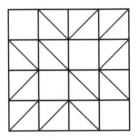

Step 5. Remove the transparent grid from your block pattern. With the **Pencil** and the thinnest line width, turn off (for Macintosh) or color double-white (for Macintosh and Windows) all pixels in horizontal or vertical grid lines that are not part of the block pattern. Zoom in and out as needed. You may use the **Eraser** sometimes, but the **Pencil** works best for fixing pixels. You can also color sets of adjoining pixels with a bucket of double-white paint if these pixels do not share an edge with any pixel that is part of the block pattern.

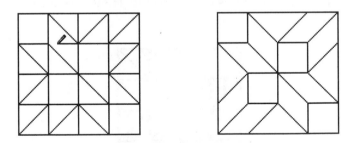

If you want to see the completed quilt block, open the file < quilt15# > in the directory < quilts# > .

Step 6. Color the various patches of the block with the **Paint Bucket**. For this example, use the two colors of any color pair combination for the parallelograms, and use double-black for the squares.

Step 7. Select **Tessellate.** *TesselMania!* generates the quiltlike tessellation by translation. The blocks are colored the same because **Tile: Same Colors** was selected in all nine grid files.

Step 8. For a different effect, select **Tile: Contrasting Colors.** This works best if you use only the two colors of any color-pair combination and, if needed, double-black.

Step 9. To make the quilt look as though it has strips of fabric (called *lattice strips*) between the blocks, reset the tile border to four pixels.

Show What You Have Learned

Recreate a quilt block (or create one of your own) using the appropriate file in the directory < sqgrids > . Color the various patches; then tessellate.

Activity 22 • Quilt Blocks and Vertex Rotation

This activity shows you how to generate a tessellation by vertex rotation. Use the tessellation from Activity 21, or open the file <quilt15> in the directory <quilts>. Return to single-tile mode. Return the tile border to the original width of two pixels (for Macintosh) or one pixel (for Windows).

Macintosh users should zoom in to **2X** magnification, use the **Marquee** to select the entire insides of the tile, select **Edit: Copy,** open the file <vrot01> in the directory <sqgrids>; then select **Edit: Paste**. Windows users need only select **Edit: Copy**, open the file <vrot01>, and then select **Edit: Paste**. Both users should then click outside the tile to deactivate the selection.

In general, use the file <vrot01> for four-by-four, five-by-five, and ten-by-ten quilt blocks; use <vrot02> for three-by-three and nine-by-nine blocks; use <vrot03> for six-by-six, eight-by-eight, and twelve-by-twelve blocks; and use <vrot04> for seven-by-seven blocks.

Select **Tessellate**. *TesselMania!* generates the tessellation by vertex rotation.

Show What You Have Learned

Create a quilt with fourfold rotational symmetry by copying and pasting a quilt block into the appropriate <vrot> file in the directory <sqgrids>.

Activity 23 • Experimenting with Color and Pattern

The colors and patterns assigned to the various patches of a quilt block have a dramatic impact on the appearance of the tessellation. You can usually set off the pattern using just three colors, but there's no maximum.

It is best to use only the two colors of any color-pair combination and, if needed, double-black if you plan to use the **Contrasting Colors** option. Or you might use a solid color and a pattern in that color instead of two colors. If you plan to keep the **Same Colors** option, the sky's the limit!

The library of quilt block patterns on pages 74 to 81 presents each block in its traditional form, with the usual number of colors (shades of gray) and the usual placement of light and dark. You can get a completely different-looking quilt if you change the location of light and dark colors. Consider the three forms of Windblown Square (quilt 12) and Double T (quilt 33) shown below.

Windblown Square

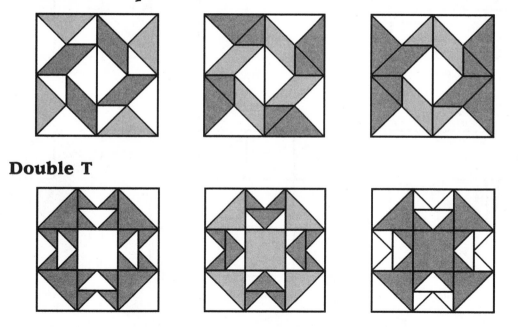

Double T

As you create your quiltlike tessellations, experiment with the color and pattern palettes, put light and dark colors in new places, and vary the transformation type using the **Copy** and **Paste** commands.

If you do not wish to draw the quilt blocks themselves, you will find a selection of ready-made blocks in the directory < quilts# >. If you need some inspiration, look at the colored quiltlike tessellations in the directory < quilts >.

Show What You Have Learned

Recreate a quilt block; then experiment with the color and pattern palettes. Vary the transformation type using the **Copy** and **Paste** commands.

Three-by-Three Blocks

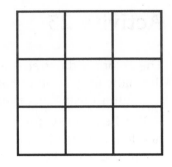

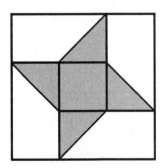

1: Split 9-Patch

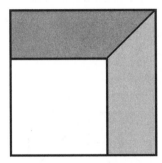

2: Attic Windows

3: Spool

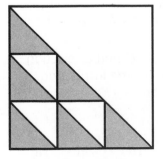

4: Friendship Star

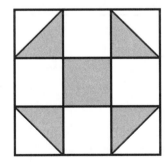

5: Shoo-Fly

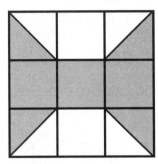

6: Maple Leaf

7: Birds-in-the-Air

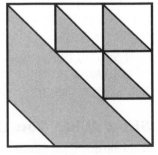

8: Formal Garden

9: Sailboat

74

Explorations with *TesselMania!*

Four-by-Four Blocks

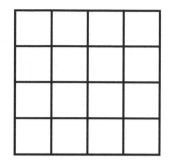

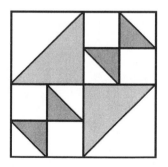

10: Yankee Puzzle

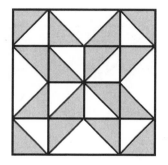

11: Pieced Star

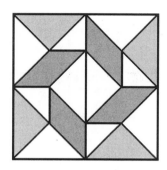

12: Windblown Square

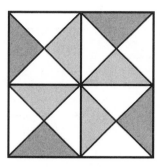

13: Crosses & Losses

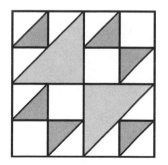

14: Old Maid's Puzzle

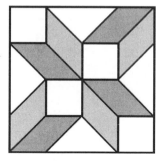

15: Cube Lattice

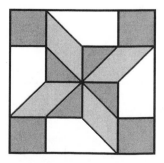

16: Clay's Choice

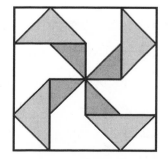

17: See Saw

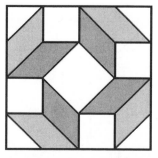

18: Bachelor's Puzzle

Five-by-Five Blocks

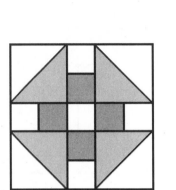
19: Churn Dash

20: Propeller

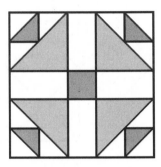
12: Duck & Ducklings

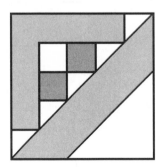
22: King's Crown

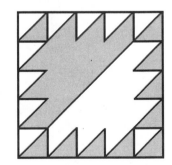
23: Lady of the Lake

24: Sawtooth

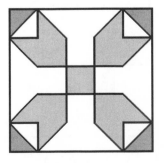
25: Fool's Square

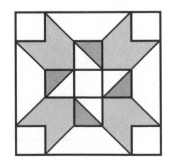
26: Quack

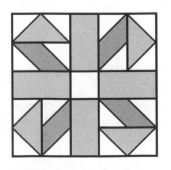
27: Jack-in-the-Box

Explorations with *TesselMania!*

Six-by-Six Blocks

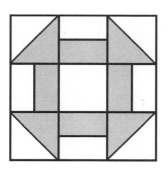

28: Sherman's March

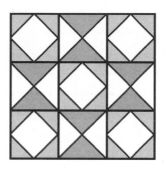

29: Combination Star

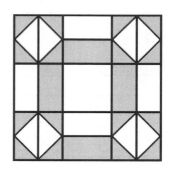

30: Rolling Stone

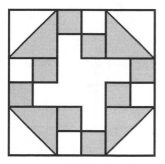

31: Prairie Queen

32: Salem, Oregon

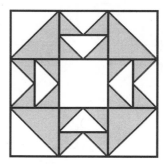

33: Double T

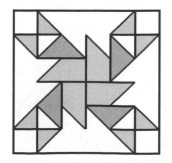

34: Rolling Pinwheel

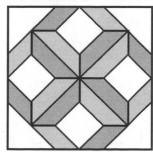

35: Shaded Trail

36: Spinning Wheel

Seven-by-Seven Blocks

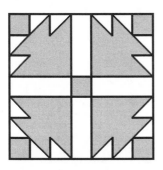

37: Dove-in-the-
Window

38: Bear's Paw

39: Maple Leaf

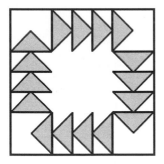

40: Wild Goose Chase

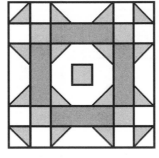

41: Greek Cross

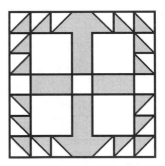

42: Hens & Chickens

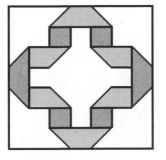

43: Twisted Ribbon

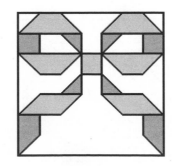

44: Ribbon Bow

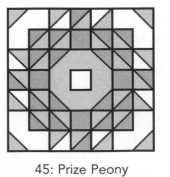

45: Prize Peony

Explorations with *TesselMania!*

Eight-by-Eight Blocks

46: Jack-in-the-Pulpit

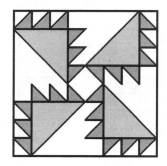

47: Indian Trails

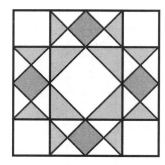

48: Square & Stars

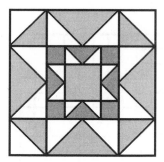

49: Eight Hands
Around

50: Carpenter's Wheel

51: Albany, New York

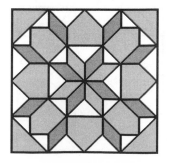

52: Jewels in a Frame

53: Odd Fellows Chain

54: Enclosed Stars

Nine-by-Nine Blocks

55: Alice's Favorite

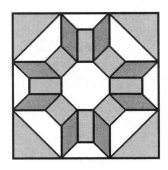

56: Prosperity Block

57: Wedding March

Ten-by-Ten Blocks

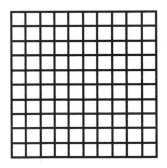

58: Katie's Favorite

59: Wood Lily

60: Bird's Nest

Twelve-by-Twelve Blocks

61: Dove at My Window

62: Chrismas Star

63: Blazing Star

Flowers and Trees

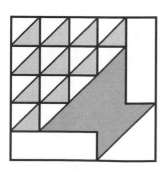

Five-by-Five

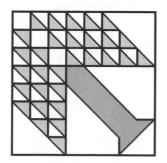

Eight-by-Eight

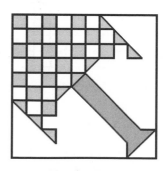

Ten-by-Ten

Square Grids

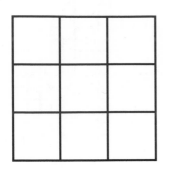

Three-by-Three

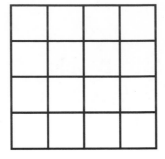

Four-by-Four

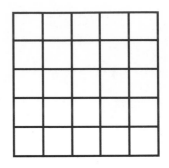

Five-by-Five

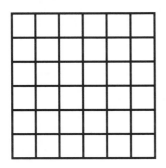

Six-by-Six

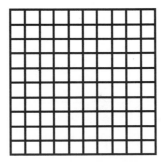

Seven-by-Seven

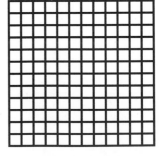

Eight-by-Eight

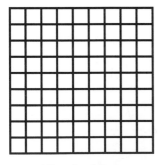

Nine-by-Nine

Ten-by-Ten

Twelve-by-Twelve

Chapter 6

Islamic Art Designs

Probably the most extensive work with tessellations was done by Moorish artists, especially between 700 A.D. and 1500 A.D. Out of devotion to their Islamic religion, the Moors did not draw human or animal forms. Instead, they used flowers and vines for their artistic inspiration. With only the most basic of tools—a compass, straightedge, and tile-cutting hammer—they used geometry to incorporate both simple and complicated patterns into their dramatic tile work.

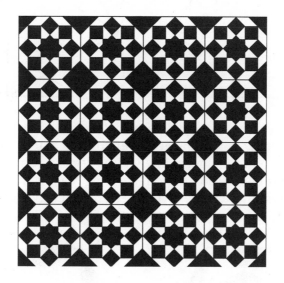

Star polygons abound in Islamic art. To create the geometrical shapes, the Moors would start with a circle, divide it into a given number of equal arcs, connect the endpoints of the arcs in some pattern, and then eliminate certain line segments.

For the final exploration with *TesselMania!,* you will recreate two kinds of Islamic designs—one based on a hexagonal star and the other on an octagonal star. Rather than start with a circle, you will start with the tessellating polygon that can envelope the star—a regular hexagon or a square.

Activity 24 • Hexagonal Star Designs

In this activity, you will recreate an Islamic design based on a hexagonal star. To save time, open the file <hexastar> in the directory <islam#> on the Explore disk. The grid on the tile was obtained by joining every vertex of a regular hexagon [Heesch type TTTTTT] to every second vertex.

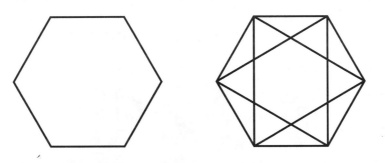

You can reconstruct any of the diagrams below using this grid. Remove any missing line segments with the **Eraser** or **Pencil.** Add any new ones with the **Line** in triple-black and the thinnest line width. Use the **Paint Bucket** to color all black regions in triple-black and the remaining regions in any colors you wish. Then select **Tessellate** to view your design. You can access colored versions of the designs in the directory <islam>.

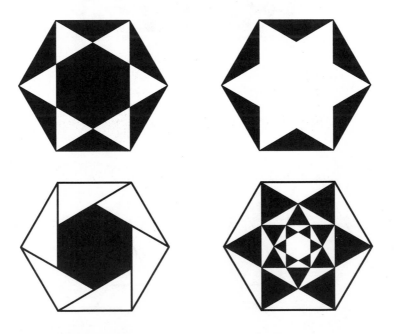

Show What You Have Learned

Recreate a hexagonal star design—or create one of your own. Explore the effect of varying color on the Islamic tessellation.

Activity 25 • Octagonal Star Designs

Another common Islamic design is based on an octagonal star. To recreate this design, begin by opening the file <octastar> in the directory <islam#>.

Select **2X** magnification. The first diagram below shows the tile grid (the circle is blue, the thin lines red). To reconstruct the second diagram, trace the octagonal star (shown in bold lines) using the **Line** in double-black and the thinnest line width. To reconstruct the third, turn off (for Macintosh) or color double-white (for Macintosh or Windows) any colored pixels that remain.

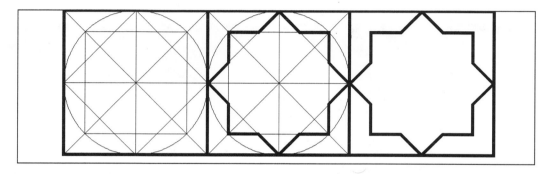

Color the regions surrounding the star in double-black with the **Paint Bucket**. You may also color the star, or leave it as is. Select **Tessellate** to view your design.

Each of the designs on the next five pages begins with the <octastar> file. The fourth is one of the eight classic semiregular tessellations. The diagrams at the top of the pages show you how to make the designs.

You can access the various tessellating blocks in the directory <islam#> and the colored versions of the Islamic designs in the directory <islam>.

Show What You Have Learned

Recreate an octagonal star design. To save time, you may begin with the file <octastar> or <octagrid> in the directory <islam#>.